IMAGES
of America

RAILROAD DEPOTS
OF SOUTHWEST OHIO

D1452012

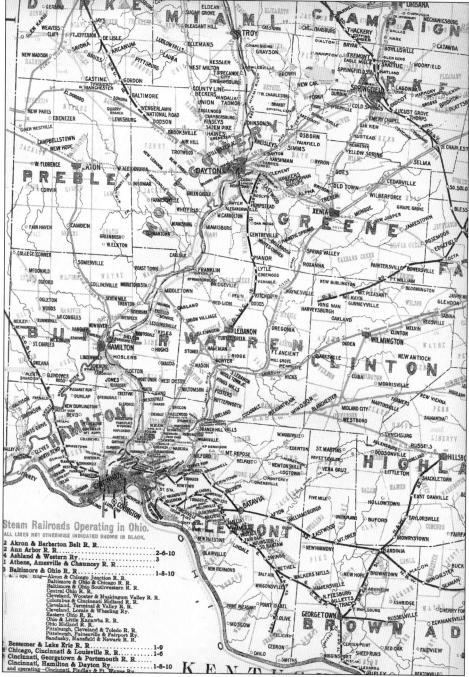

This map shows the railroads of Southwest Ohio in 1909. (Ohio Railroad Commission.)

ON THE COVER: It is a pleasant summer day in Williamsburg around 1907. What better place for small-town children to be than down at the depot waiting for the arrival of the next passenger train. The Williamsburg depot dates to around 1900 and was constructed by the Norfolk and Western Railway. (Author's collection.)

IMAGES
of America

RAILROAD DEPOTS
OF SOUTHWEST OHIO

Mark J. Camp

ARCADIA
PUBLISHING

Published by Arcadia Publishing
Charleston, South Carolina

Printed in the United States of America

Library of Congress Control Number: 2010920067

For all general information contact Arcadia Publishing at:
Telephone 843-853-2070
Fax 843-853-0044
E-mail sales@arcadiapublishing.com
For customer service and orders:
Toll-Free 1-888-313-2665

Visit us on the Internet at www.arcadiapublishing.com

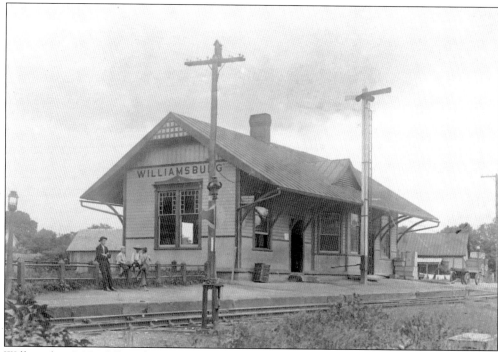

Williamsburg's Norfolk and Western (N&W) depot serves as a model for a typical small town combination depot. A general waiting room is in the left end of the building. The bay window or vestibule marks the agent's office. On the far side of the depot is the freight room. The semaphore signal outside the office is called an order board. The agent could move the blades up or down from inside the office, indicating what the train crew needed to do—for example, stop for passengers and/or orders, proceed without stopping, pick up freight, or stop because of problems ahead. The ladder was used for maintenance of the order board and to light the lantern at the top for night use. Note also the platform lanterns and ever-present baggage wagon. (Author's collection.)

CONTENTS

ACKNOWLEDGMENTS

I appreciate the contribution of photographs and data from the following individuals and organizations: Baltimore and Ohio Historical Society, Baltimore and Ohio Railroad Museum, Chesapeake and Ohio Historical Society, Cincinnati Museum Center, Public Library of Cincinnati and Hamilton County, Cincinnati Railroad Club, Dayton Metro Library, Dan E. Finfrock, Wendell McChord, Middletown Public Library, Norfolk and Western Railway Historical Society, Norfolk-Southern Corporation, David P. Oroszi, Pennsylvania Railroad Technical and Historical Society, Gary D. Rolih, Stephen B. Smalley, Smith Library of Regional History, Toledo-Lucas County Public Library, the University of Toledo Carlson Library, the Virginia Tech University Library, and to many others credited in the photograph captions. All have contributed in some way, through words, maps, photographs, or inspiration; some recently, some many years ago.

I have also found the following references useful for telling the story of Ohio depots: Robert L. Black's *The Little Miami Railroad*; Jim Blount's *Railroads of Butler County*; George H. Burgess and Miles C. Kennedy's *Centennial History of the Pennsylvania Railroad Company 1846–1946*; the Cincinnati Railroad Club's *Cincinnati Union Terminal: the Design and Construction of an Art Deco Masterpiece*; Carl W. Condit's *The Railroad and the City*; John R. Grabb's *The Marietta and Cincinnati Railroad, and its Successor—The Baltimore and Ohio: The Study of this once Great Route Across Ohio 1851–1988*; Alvin F. Harlow's *The Road of the Century*; John W. Hauck's *Narrow Gauge in Ohio The Cincinnati, Lebanon and Northern Railway*; David McNeil's *Railroad With Three Gauges The Cincinnati, Georgetown and Portsmouth RR and Felicity and Bethel Railroad*; various volumes of the Ohio Railway Report and Poors Manuals; John A. Rehor's *The Nickel Plate Story*; *Dayton, Ohio Railroad History—Summary* compiled by Kirk Reynolds and David P. Oroszi; various issues of *The Sentinel*; Stephen B. Smalley's *The Cincinnati, Georgetown and Portsmouth Railroad*; Robert F. Smith's *From the Ohio to the Mississippi A Story of a Railroad*; Rick Tipton and Chuck Blardone's *The Pennsylvania Railroad in Cincinnati*; Scott D. Trostel's *The Detroit, Toledo and Ironton Railroad Henry Ford's Railroad*; John H. White Jr.'s *On the Right Track Some Historic Cincinnati Railroads*, and various railroad trade journals.

INTRODUCTION

Southwest Ohio's early growth was tied to the Ohio River and its tributaries and, by the 1830s, to the Miami and Erie Canal. However, the laying of the first iron-sheathed wooden rails into riverfront Cincinnati in the late 1830s was a harbinger of the railroad boom to come—an event that would change the way goods were moved for the next century. The first rails in Southwest Ohio belonged to the Little Miami Railroad, incorporated in 1836. Building a railroad in this part of the state was not easy; bedrock was close to the surface, and the only level ground was either near the streams and rivers or on top of the hills. The Little Miami Railroad built up the Ohio Valley to Columbia and then north up the west side of the Little Miami River Valley. The initial plan was to meet the Mad River and Lake Erie Railroad, building southwest from Sandusky on Lake Erie, at Springfield. By the time the Mad River Line reached Springfield, the Little Miami Railroad found that a connection at Xenia with the associated Columbus and Xenia Railroad offered even more opportunity.

Many early lines in Southwest Ohio opened as narrow-gauge railroads where the rails were 3 feet apart, instead of the 4 feet, 8 inches of standard gauge. Until the 1890s, there was a plan to link many of the narrow-gauge companies into a great narrow-gauge network extending throughout the Midwest. Adding interest to the railroads of southwest counties was the presence of wide-gauge lines, like the Atlantic and Great Western Railway and the Ohio and Mississippi Railroad (both 6 feet between the rails). The Cincinnati and Hamilton Railroad had still a different gauge—4 feet, 10 inches between the rails.

From a city so fearful that the newfangled steam locomotives would scare the horses that the city fathers forbade the locomotives in the downtown—instead requiring them to stop around Pendleton and let horses and mules pull the stagecoach-like cars into the city center—Cincinnati soon became a rail center. Railroad lines fanning out from Cincinnati, Dayton, and Springfield, and those connecting the towns along the Miami River Valley, led to development of suburban communities. As workers moved from the city centers, commuter passenger service became important. The railroad depot became the focal point of many towns. In the big cities, the depot became symbolic of the railroad company, and considerable emphasis was placed on designing an attractive structure—one that would draw more patrons. As Cincinnati and Dayton grew, it became favorable to construct union depots where the populace could conveniently board whichever line best served their travel plans, rather than seeking out separate, sometimes widely separated, depots. Separate freight and baggage stations were also typical of the big city. Separate passenger and freight depots were also erected in smaller cities like Hamilton and Middletown and in other towns where business was heavy. Smaller communities were well served by the classic combination depot where passenger, freight, and baggage facilities were combined under one roof.

By the 1890s, hundreds of southeast Ohio communities depended on their depot or depots for daily news delivered by telegraph and train travelers, shipments from catalog companies, domestic and commercial mail, commercial freight for local stores, vacation and business trips, daily commuting, and visits to friends and relatives. The Baltimore and Ohio, Chesapeake and Ohio, Erie, Louisville and Nashville, New York Central, Norfolk and Western, Pennsylvania, and Southern Railroads were the major players in Southwest Ohio by the 1920s. The Golden Age of rail travel lasted until the war years; then the increasing use of autos, buses, and trucks led to closing of depots and a reduction in passenger service. The last major depot construction in this part of Ohio was the erection of Cincinnati Union Terminal and a new Pennsylvania Railroad passenger depot at Norwood in the 1930s and the reconstruction of Dayton Union Station and erection of a new New York Central passenger depot at Middletown in the 1960s. Today only a few hundred depots remain in the entire state, and most of the survivors are serving some nonrailroad function.

A number of shorter railroad lines once served southeast Ohio, including the Cincinnati and Westwood, College Hill, Felicity and Bethel, and Ohio River and Columbus. The Cincinnati and Westwood became a commuter line extending 8 miles from Glenmore into the Cincinnati, Hamilton, and Dayton (CH&D) depot in downtown Cincinnati. The College Hill Railroad, later the Cincinnati Northwestern Railway, served commuters along its 14-mile route to Mount Healthy. A photographic record of these short line depots appears to be mostly lacking.

The vast majority of depots pictured in the coming chapters have long since disappeared from the Ohio wayside. Some burned or were damaged beyond repair in train derailments. Most were simply removed by the railroad companies after their usefulness ended, especially when abandonment led to neglect and vandalism. Some were sold or given away with the condition they be moved off railroad property. Brookville, Franklin, Germantown, Glendale, Lewisburg, Trotwood, and Winton Place have been restored and serve as historical museums and/or community centers. Cincinnati Union Terminal is now Cincinnati Museum Center and houses the Cincinnati Museum of Natural History, the Cincinnati Historical Society museum and library, and the Cincinnati Railroad Club. Eaton, Elmwood Place, Loveland, Madeira, Miamisburg, Middletown, Milford, Morrow, Norwood, and West Middletown now house businesses. Camden, Farmersville, Lindenwald, West Alexandria, Whitfield, and Woods have been converted to residences. Depots at Hamilton, Oakley, and St. Bernard remain in railroad storage and maintenance use. Norwood's Pennsylvania Railroad depot and the Cincinnati, Georgetown, and Portsmouth (CG&P) Railroad depot at Mount Washington now house fraternal organizations. For an updated list of remaining depots and other railroad and interurban structures please visit the Web site of the Railroad Station Historical Society at www.rrshs.org.

This book is an attempt to present some vintage views of a selection of the depots that played an important role in the development of many villages, towns, and cities in Southwest Ohio. It is also a look at the big city depots and the many commuter depots in the suburbs around Cincinnati.

One

BALTIMORE AND OHIO LINES

The Cincinnati, Hamilton, and Dayton opened between the namesakes in fall 1851. In 1863, the CH&D entered into a lease agreement with the Dayton and Michigan Railroad, which had begun construction at Dayton north to Toledo in 1852. The Junction Railroad completed a line from Hamilton to Oxford by 1859 and eventually reached Indianapolis, but financial difficulties led to its reorganization as the Cincinnati, Hamilton, and Indianapolis in 1872 under CH&D control. The CH&D also controlled the former Eaton and Hamilton Railroad, which ran between Hamilton and Richmond, Indiana, between 1866 and 1888 and the Louisville, Cincinnati, and Dayton Railroad, which in 1887 opened from Middletown to Hamilton. Narrow-gauge trains were running on the Dayton and Southeastern Railroad by 1877 between Dayton and Washington Court House and on the Dayton, Covington, and Toledo Railroad from Stillwater Junction to West Milton in 1879. Both lines eventually were converted to standard gauge and passed under CH&D control by 1891. The Baltimore and Ohio Railroad (B&O) took over operation of all remaining CH&D lines in 1917.

The Marietta and Cincinnati (M&C) Railroad (formerly the Belpre and Cincinnati Railroad) completed the Cincinnati end of its line in fall 1854. The original terminus was Loveland and a connection with the Little Miami line, which carried M&C passengers into Cincinnati. This arrangement continued into the late 1860s when the M&C bridged the Little Miami River at Loveland and built its own line into downtown Cincinnati. The M&C became a B&O property in 1882 and merged into the B&O Southwestern in 1889. Cincinnati gained another line when the Ohio and Mississippi Railroad began construction down the Ohio River Valley in 1852. Hoping to interchange with the Atlantic and Great Western Railroad, the O&M was built to broad gauge—6 feet between the rails. The stretch from Cincinnati to Seymour, Indiana, was completed in 1854. The company converted to standard gauge in the summer of 1871 and became part of the B&O Southwestern in 1893.

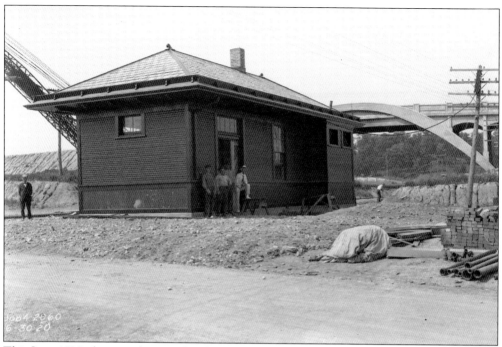

This June 1920 photograph was taken by Miami Valley Conservancy officials while designing flood control projects in the Dayton area. It shows a newly constructed B&O combination depot on the relocated former Cincinnati, Hamilton, and Dayton line at Vandalia. This was a popular depot plan; depots of this design were built at many stations on the entire B&O system. Before the realignment, the CH&D depot at Tadmor served passengers from Vandalia. (Miami Conservancy District photograph.)

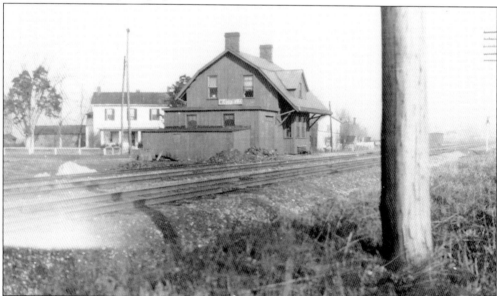

Whitfield was served by this two-story depot with living quarters for the agent on the second floor as shown in this *c.* 1917 photograph. The depot remains as a residence. (B&O Railroad photograph, the Hays T. Watkins Research Library, B&O Museum, Inc.)

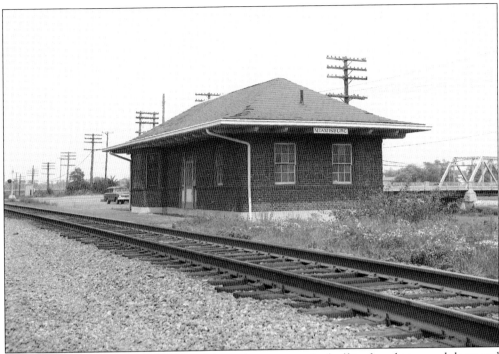

An earlier CH&D passenger depot in Miamisburg was washed off its foundation and destroyed during the 1913 flood. The B&O replaced it with this brick depot. The depot is still used by CSX. (Photograph by the author.)

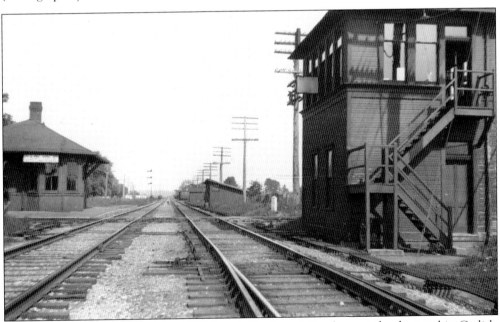

The joint passenger depot of the CH&D and Cincinnati Northern at the diamond in Carlisle is seen in this northern view up the CH&D dating to the early 1900s. Across the diamond is a frame B&O design interlocking tower. Pipes control the interlocking signals at the crossing. All are now gone. (Dan E. Finfrock collection.)

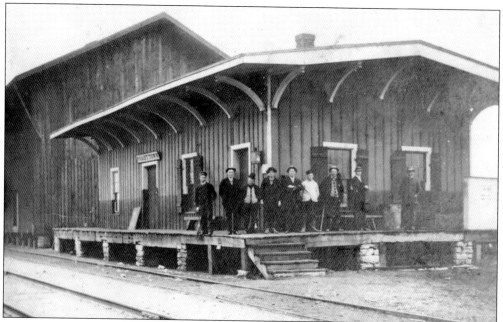

Poast Town's depot dates to at least the 1860s. The CH&D completed their line through here in 1851. Behind this passenger depot is a large freight house that also provided an area to store grain. (Middletown Public Library collection.)

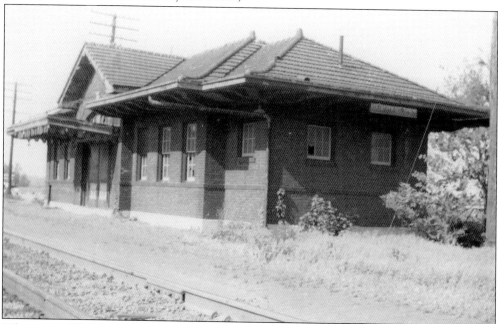

When the CH&D built through Middletown, they stayed west of the Great Miami River. Brick passenger and freight depots replaced an 1851 frame depot sometime in the 1870s–1880s. The second passenger depot was destroyed and the freight house damaged in the 1913 flood. This passenger depot, built to B&O plans, replaced the washed away structure in 1914. The last passenger train left in 1971, and the depot was demolished shortly after. The freight house still stands. (Author's collection.)

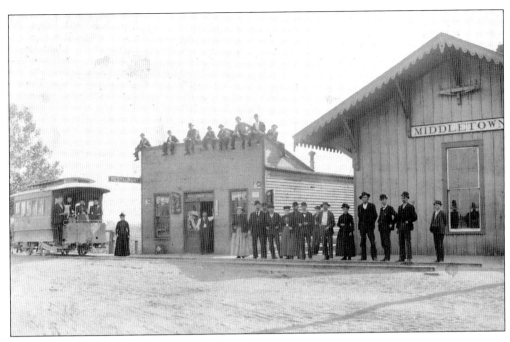

Downtown Middletown was served by the above frame depot after a CH&D line was built up the east side of the Great Miami River from Hamilton in 1889. A horse-drawn trolley line connected the Middletown depots of the CH&D and the Cleveland, Columbus, Cincinnati, and Indianapolis Railroad, or CCC&I. By 1910, this depot had been replaced by the passenger depot below. By the 1970s, only a frame freight station remained on this line. (Both, Middletown Public Library collection.)

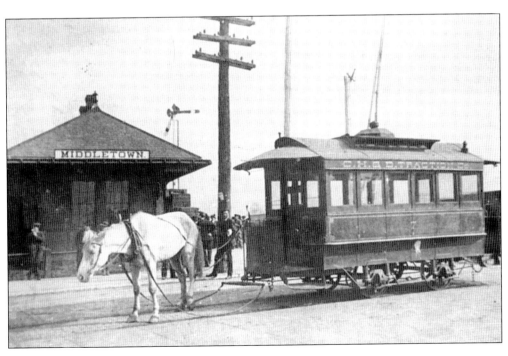

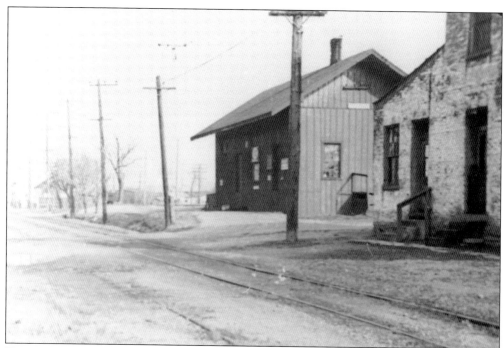

Trenton was served by this CH&D depot. In the early 1900s, the Cincinnati and Lake Erie traction line erected its depot next door where it crossed the CH&D. This view dates from 1938–1939. (Dan E. Finfrock collection.)

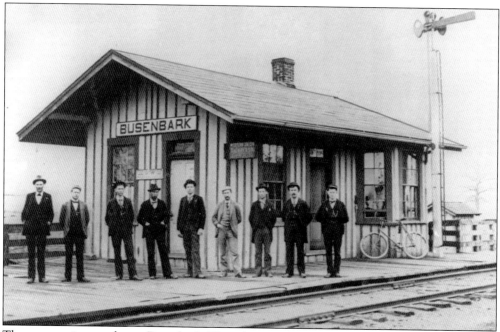

The next station south was Busenbark. This photograph dates to September 5, 1897. The men are, from left to right, Charles Whitman, Henry N. Wagner (night operator), Samuel B. Hine, Jay Warwick, William Featherland, William Warner, Hans Schmitt, Ed Richter, and Harry Kline (day operator). (Dan E. Finfrock collection.)

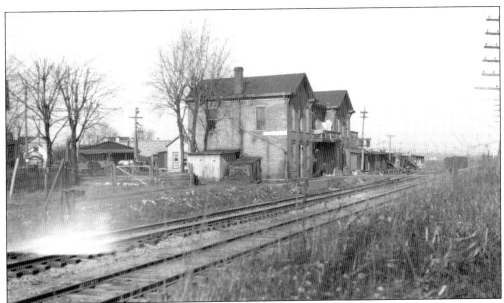

According to the 1875 *Butler County Atlas*, J. E. Overpeck's mill and blacksmith shop served as the Overpeck depot in the early days. The CH&D depot and office building is pictured from 1918. Divisional offices were located here in the late 1800s. The CH&D maintained yards just south of here. (B&O Railroad photograph, the Hays T. Watkins Research Library, B&O Museum, Inc.)

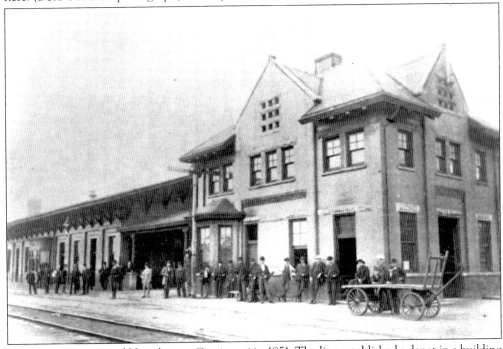

The CH&D connected Hamilton to Cincinnati in 1851. The line established a depot in a building at the corner of South Fourth and Caldwell Streets. The CH&D then built a brick and stone depot at South Fifth and Henry Streets, probably just after the Civil War. By 1878, thirty-five passenger trains passed through town each day. In 1885–1886, the CH&D built a two-story addition on one end. (Author's collection.)

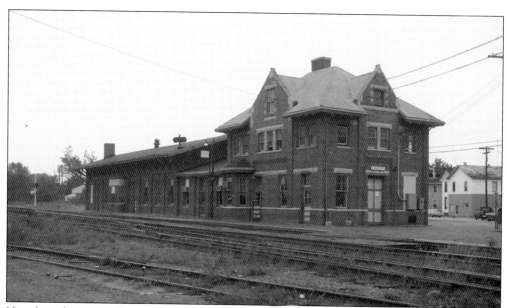

Hamilton depot was shared with the Cincinnati, Indianapolis, and Western (CI&W) Railroad (the former Junction Railroad). In 1920, Hamilton entertained a plan to build an elaborate union station involving the B&O, CI&W, and the Pennsylvania Railroad, or PRR. It did not get beyond the paper stage. The plans were resurrected in the 1930s and 1940s, but the only result was the construction of the High Street underpass. April 30, 1971, marked the departure of the last B&O passenger train. This view dates to September 1971. (Photograph by Charles Garvin.)

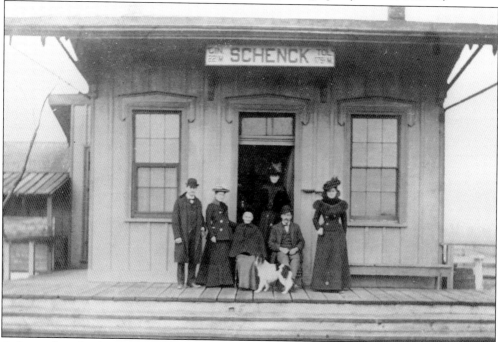

A depot of similar design to Whitfield once served Lindenwald. It still remains in residential use. The next station south was Schencks. This depot was located where present State Route 4 passes under the CSX main line in Fairfield. (Dan E. Finfrock collection.)

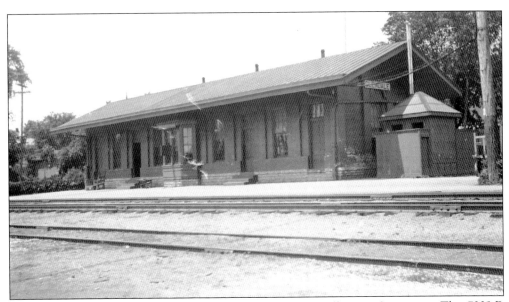

Glendale more or less marks the start of major commuter traffic into Cincinnati. The CH&D erected a number of impressive depots from here to the Queen city. The brick depot in this 1918 image dates to 1880, the third depot at the site. The first depot was a small frame structure. The second depot, a much larger building, burned down. By the mid-1960s, Glendale's depot had been converted to business use. It now serves as a museum. (B&O Railroad photograph, the Hays T. Watkins Research Library, B&O Museum, Inc.)

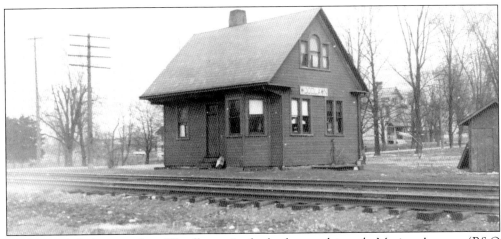

In this c. 1918 photograph is Woodlawn. In the background is early Marion Avenue. (B&O Railroad photograph, the Hays T. Watkins Research Library, B&O Museum, Inc.)

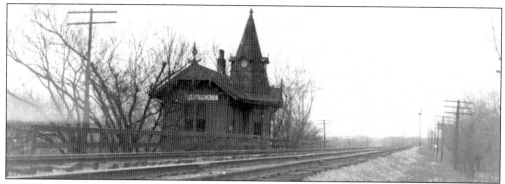

Park Place's ornate passenger depot reflected the stately homes in this suburb. It was built high on the bank of Mill Creek. A bridge connected the depot to the Park Place development. It disappeared at an early date. (Dan E. Finfrock collection.)

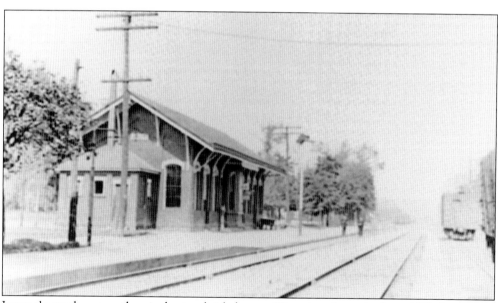

Just to the south was another single-story brick depot at Wyoming, shown in this c. 1918 photograph, also dating to the 1870s. (B&O Railroad photograph, the Hays T. Watkins Research Library, B&O Museum, Inc.)

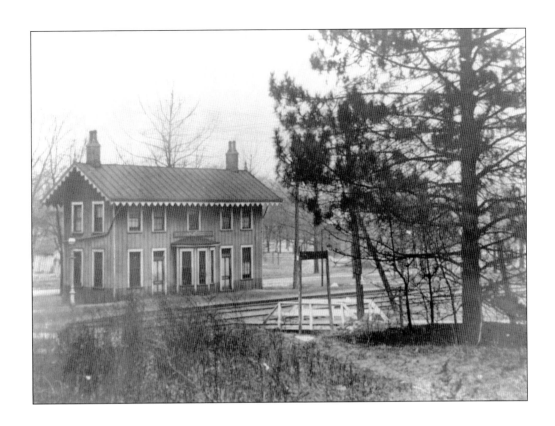

The depots at the next two towns, Maplewood and Hartwell, were two-story frame buildings with second-floor living quarters for the agent. At Maplewood (above), a CH&D branch served Lockland to the east. The lower right-hand part of the depot housed an ice cream shop at one time run by the live-in agent. The Hartwell depot (below) also had second-floor living quarters for its agent. It stood in the southwest corner where Parkway Avenue crossed the tracks. (Above, author's collection; below, c. 1918 B&O Railroad photograph, the Hays T. Watkins Research Library, B&O Museum, Inc.)

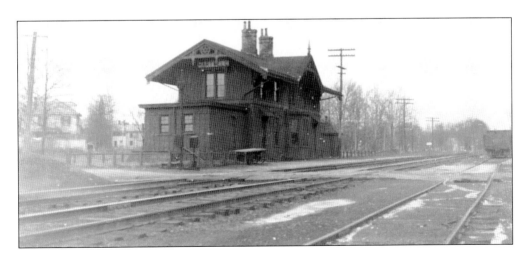

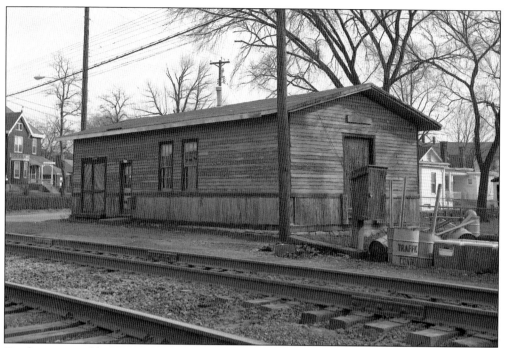

Carthage is an old community and once was the home to the Longview Lunatic Asylum. This slightly modified second generation B&O combination depot still stands at Carthage. Although modified for strictly freight use by the mid-1900s, it originally handled passengers as well. This view shows the depot still in storage use by the railroad in January 1973. (Photograph by the author.)

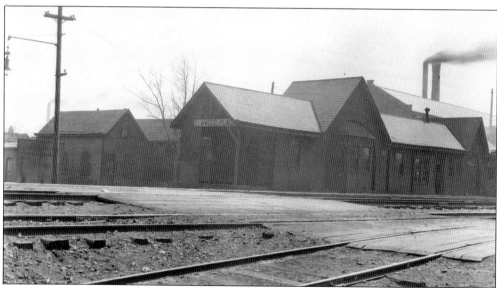

Around 1918, this combination depot served the commuters of Elmwood Place. The Cleveland, Cincinnati, Chicago, and St. Louis Railway, commonly known as the "Big Four," also had a depot on the other side of town. (B&O Railroad photograph, the Hays T. Watkins Research Library, B&O Museum, Inc.)

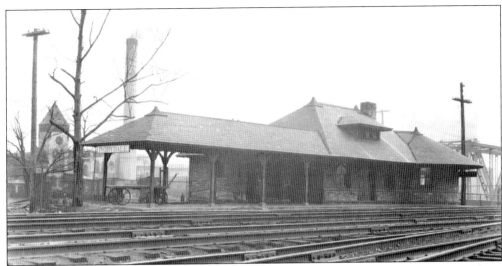

A stone passenger depot at Ivorydale was built by the Proctor and Gamble Company, whose large plant sprawled behind the depot. One of William Proctor's (the 1837 founder) sons lived in Glendale and commuted daily to this depot. He saw to it that a suitable passenger depot was built. The railroad just leased it from the company. When the railroad discontinued service to Ivorydale, the depot was demolished. (c. 1918 B&O Railroad photograph, the Hays T. Watkins Research Library, B&O Museum, Inc.)

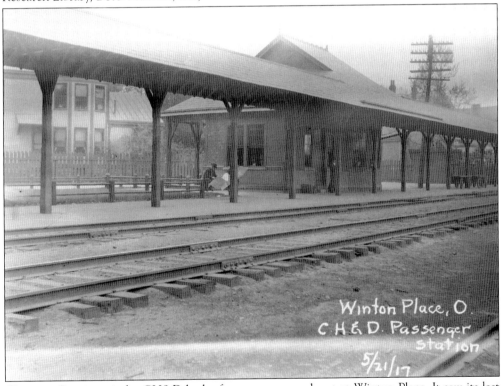

Closer to Cincinnati, the CH&D had a frame passenger depot at Winton Place. It saw its last passengers in 1933 with the opening of Cincinnati Union Terminal. (B&O Railroad photograph, the Hays T. Watkins Research Library, B&O Museum, Inc.)

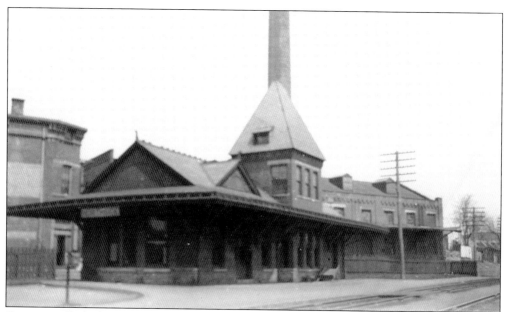

Cumminsville had two active CH&D passenger depots until the opening of Cincinnati Union Terminal in 1933. On the north edge of town was Northside depot (above), and on the south end was Southside (below). There were also two depots on the old Marietta and Cincinnati and one on the Dayton Short Line. The next CH&D depot was in Brighton. (Above, author's collection; below, c. 1918 B&O Railroad photograph, the Hays T. Watkins Research Library, B&O Museum, Inc.)

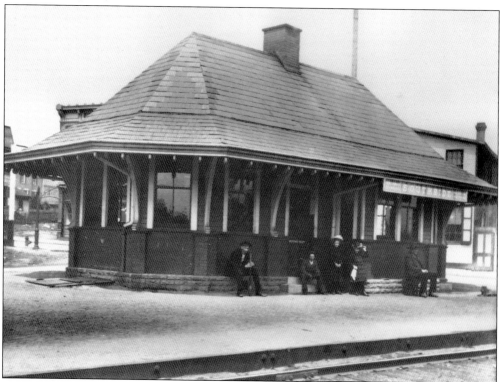

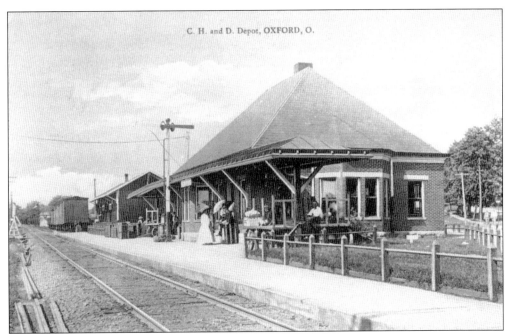

The first depot in Oxford was a long frame structure constructed by the Junction Railroad in 1859. This unpretentious building became the freight house when the new brick passenger depot, shown above, was opened in 1896. Newly revitalized Miami University and neighboring Oxford College and the Western welcomed the new facilities. The new depot was located on South Elm Street. This 1910 postal view shows both depots. The last scheduled passenger train left December 16, 1950. The once important college-town depot was razed in 1994. (Author's collection.)

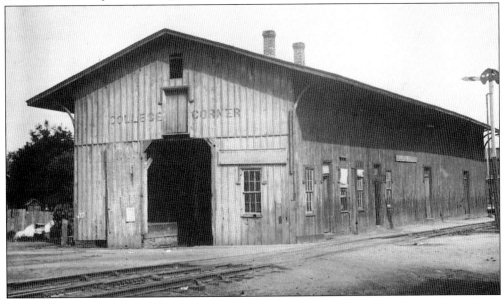

The Junction Railroad's depot at College Corner was a classic example of pre–Civil War depot design. The passengers loaded on the near side of this depot, while freight was handled inside the barn-like building. Note the doors in the eave, allowing transfer of grain from the loft. (Gary D. Rolih collection.)

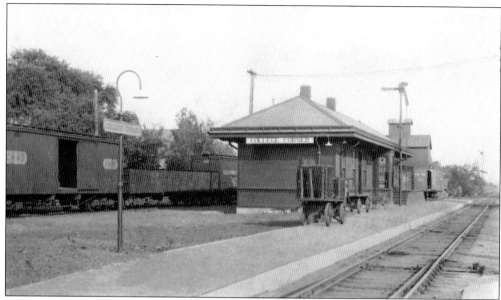

After the Cincinnati, Hamilton, and Dayton came under Baltimore and Ohio control, this standard design B&O combination depot was built on the same site as the older College Corner depot. The gooseneck platform light with cast iron town board was a common embellishment of B&O depots. (Gary D. Rolih collection.)

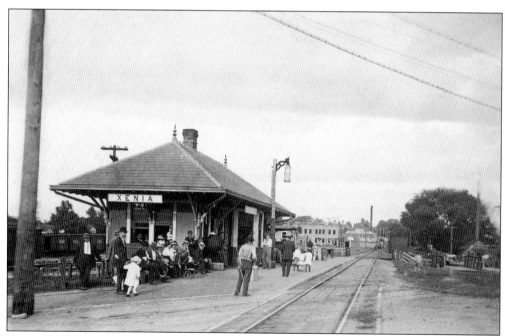

Xenia welcomed its third railroad line in the 1870s, when the narrow-gauge Dayton and Southeastern built through on its way to the coalfields. After the CH&D gained control and the line was converted to standard gauge, the above passenger depot was completed at Xenia. A separate freight house was constructed nearby. Only the freight house remained in the 1970s. (Gary D. Rolih collection.)

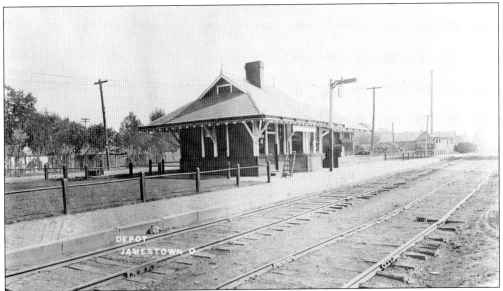

Farther east on the line at Jamestown, the Cincinnati, Hamilton, and Dayton built this combination depot in the 1890s, replacing an earlier structure. This particular design was widely used on the CH&D lines. (Author's collection.)

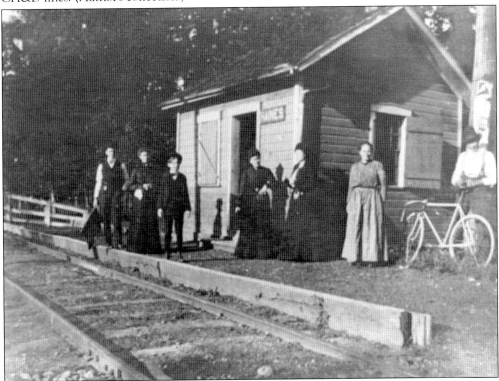

Another narrow-gauge line that eventually came under CH&D control was the Dayton, Covington, and Toledo Railroad. The first station north of Stillwater Junction was Haines, located at the crossing of the Dayton and Northern Traction. This non-agency depot is long gone. (David P. Oroszi collection.)

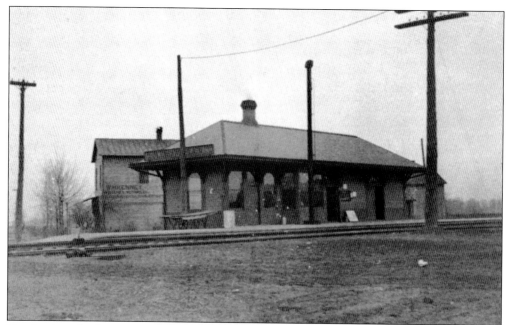

Coming into the Cincinnati region from the east is the line of the former Marietta and Cincinnati (M&C) Railroad, later part of the Baltimore and Ohio Southwestern line. The depot at Pleasant Plain fits a standard B&O design of the early 1900s. This replaced an earlier depot built by the M&C. (Gary D. Rolih collection.)

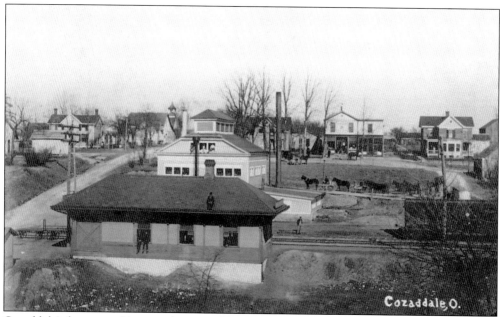

Cozaddale's frame combination depot is of B&OSW design. The Cozaddale Creamery, directly across the tracks from the depot, was the main shipper in town. It is obvious that the residents knew that this was the day that a photographer was going to record views of the community. Note the lineup of farm wagons at the creamery and the man on the roof of the depot. (Gary D. Rolih collection.)

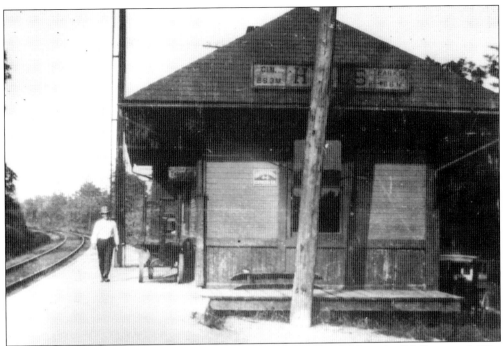

The Hills depot probably dates from the 1880s after the M&C fell under B&O control. The town-board design marks this as a B&OSW property of the early 1900s. The agent walks the platform readying for the next train. Behind the depot is a horse-drawn omnibus waiting to take passengers to the local hotel. (Dan E. Finfrock collection.)

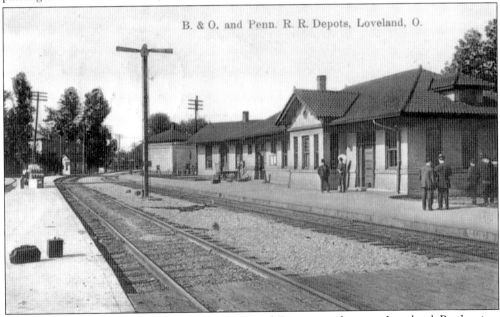

The B&OSW used an earlier depot of Marietta and Cincinnati design at Loveland. By the time of this c. 1910 postal card view, the depot had been replaced with this structure. Loveland was at the eastern edge of the B&O commuter district in the early 1900s. The adjacent depot served the Pennsylvania Railroad. (Gary D. Rolih collection.)

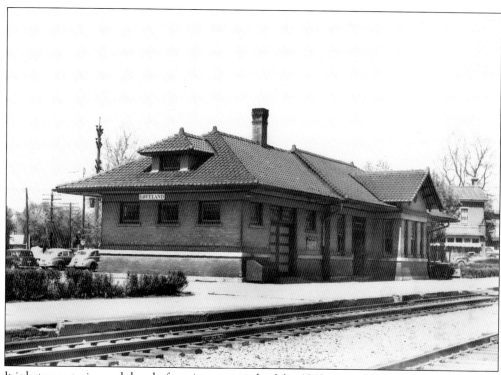

It is between trains and the platform is empty in this May 1949 view of the 1907 Loveland depot. Also at this junction, to the left of this view, was the old Little Miami depot. The B&O depot is the only survivor, now under business use. (Cincinnati Railroad Club collection.)

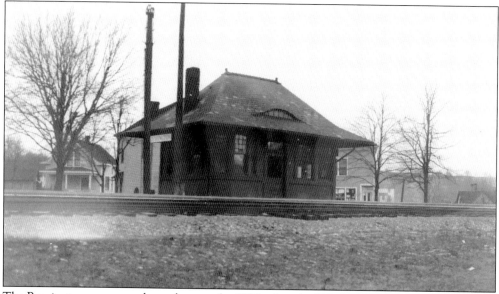

The Remington passenger depot dates to the 1880s after the M&C came under B&O control. It was a busy place in the morning and late afternoon, when commuters filled the platform. (c. 1918 B&O Railroad photograph, the Hays T. Watkins Research Library, B&O Museum, Inc.)

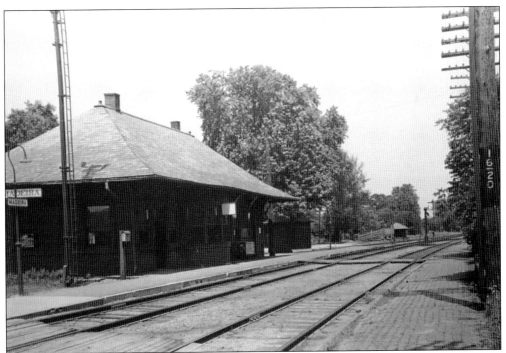

Madeira depot has a rounded bay window and exceedingly tall order board, distinguishing it from others in the Cincinnati commuting district. Madeira depot, located on Railroad Avenue, reportedly dates to around 1870. After closing in July 1972, it has been converted to business use. The next station west was at Allandale. Although a rather small frame building, the depot did have a bay window. (Cincinnati Railroad Club collection.)

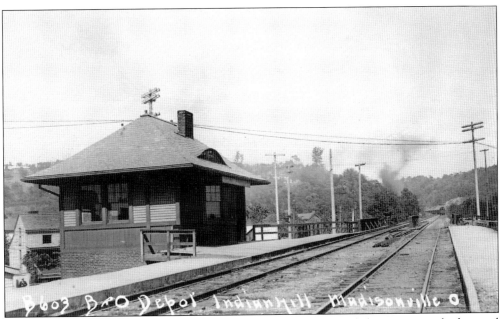

The Baltimore & Ohio Southwestern, later just B&O, maintained this interestingly designed commuter depot at East Madisonville in the early 1900s. (Gary D. Rolih collection.)

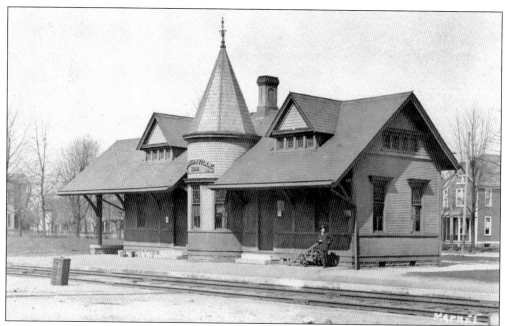

The Madisonville depot was constructed in 1888 by the B&O Southwestern and is more typical of B&O depots in the eastern states. Note the town name and building date are embossed on the conical tower. (Author's collection.)

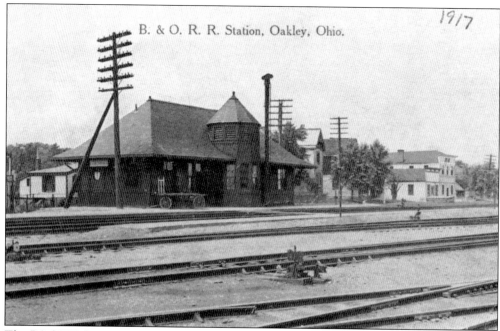

The B&OSW depot in Oakley reportedly dates to 1871. In the early 1900s, the above depot sported an ornamental tower over the telegrapher's bay. In later years, during a modernization program of the B&O, the tower was removed. The depot remains on Enyart Street, used most recently for storage by the railroad. (Gary D. Rolih collection.)

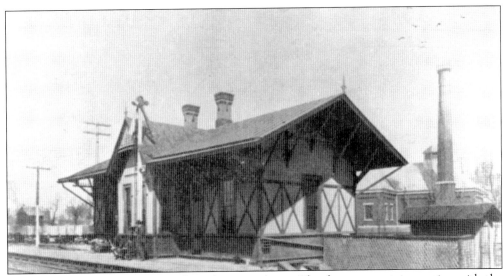

Above is an earlier East Norwood combination depot. The depot was a joint station with the Cincinnati, Lebanon, and Northern Railroad beginning in 1881. It was replaced by the below depot, constructed to a standard plan of the B&OSW with a tower inserted in the middle to control the interlocking with the CL&N. By the early 1970s, the freight end of the building had been removed and replaced with a separate brick structure. The former depot had become strictly a tower. A fire damaged the structure in May 2000. Norwood's main depot, a former Marietta and Cincinnati structure, was further west. (Above, Dan E. Finfrock collection; below, Cincinnati Railroad Club collection.)

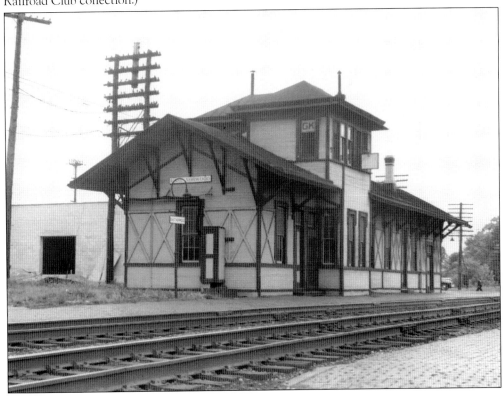

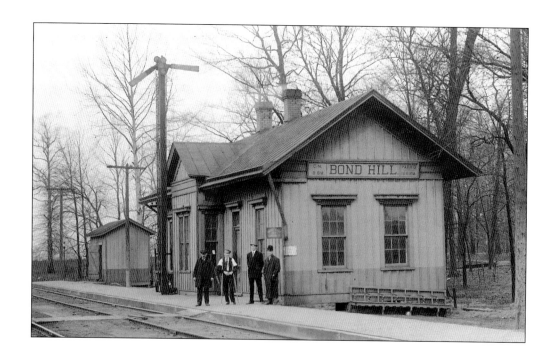

Bond Hill, above, was served by this frame combination depot dating to the 1870s. Below is the St. Bernard B&OSW passenger depot. Later the depot's decorative continuation of the circular bay window above the roof was removed, and windows and doors were rearranged. For clearance, the roof overhang on the trackside was cut back. Nearby was NA Tower at Ivorydale Junction. St. Bernard depot and the newer brick NA Tower remain. (Above, Gary D. Rolih collection; below, c. 1918 B&O Railroad photograph, the Hays T. Watkins Research Library, B&O Museum, Inc.)

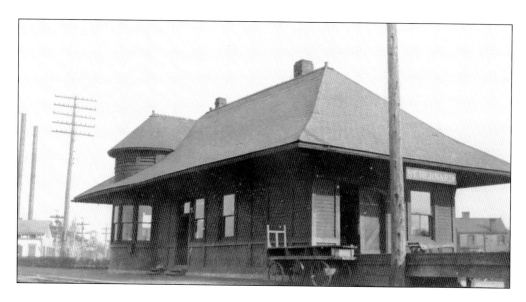

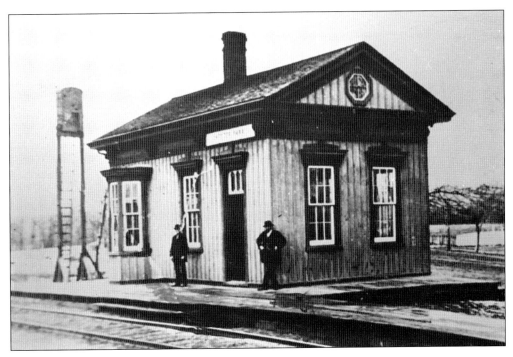

The above photograph depicts the Marietta and Cincinnati passenger depot at Chester Park in 1873. The c. 1865 depot still sports the old-style order board. Below is the same depot in 1966 after a rebuilding around 1890 and a renaming of the community to Winton Place. The depot was on the north side of the tracks along with a small freight shed. Across the tracks was a three-sided passenger shelter. In later years, the depot was painted University of Cincinnati colors—red and black. The depot was moved to Sharon Woods Metro Park and nicely restored. (Both, author's collection.)

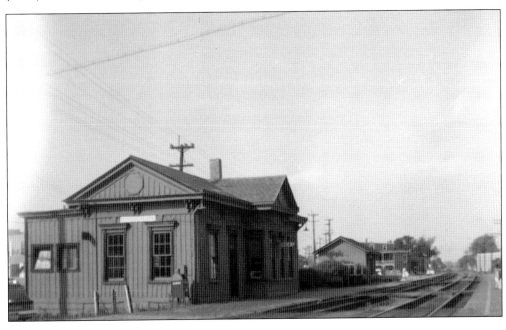

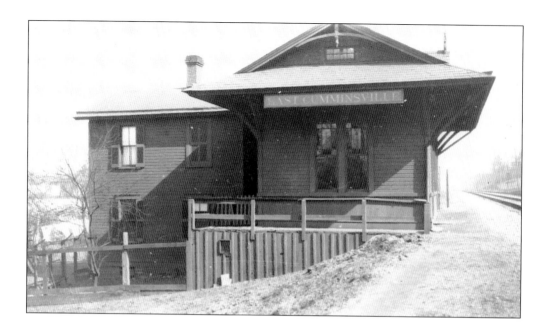

Cumminsville had four passenger depots. Besides two CH&D depots, the community was served by the above B&O depot at East Cumminsville, less than a mile beyond Winton Place. The station agent's house is directly behind the depot. Less than half a mile west was the main Cumminsville depot, shown below. The brick structure was located at Apple Street and Vandalia Avenue. (Both, c. 1918 B&O Railroad photographs, the Hays T. Watkins Research Library, B&O Museum, Inc.)

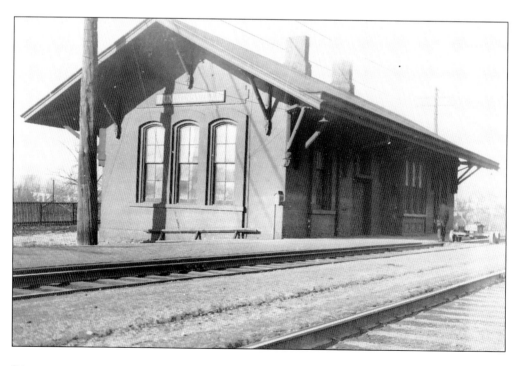

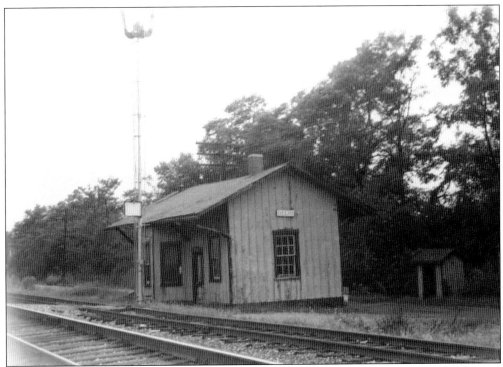

On the west side of Cincinnati, the B&O followed the Ohio River to the Indiana border and then on to St. Louis. The B&O depot at Delhi is shown in September 1966. It was built during the B&OSW era along the old Ohio and Mississippi Railroad. Being on the floodplain of the Ohio River, the depot was occasionally under water. The Delhi depot was gone by the 1970s. The B&OSW depot at North Bend was also on the river side of the tracks and was probably destroyed in the 1913 flood. (Above, photograph by Max Miller; below, Gary D. Rolih collection.)

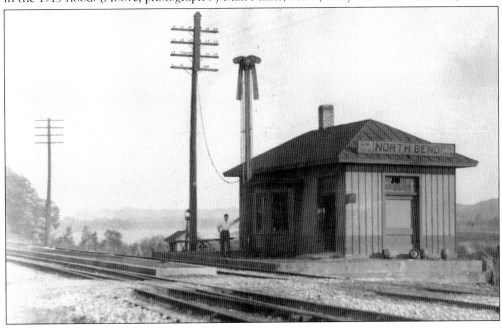

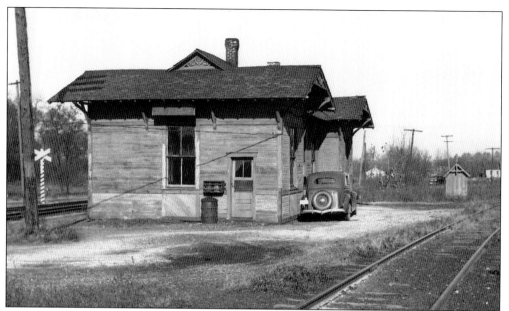

Durbin was where the Erie crossed the Big Four just west of Springfield. This frame depot served as a joint depot in the early years. By the early 1970s, it had been shortened by the New York Central Railroad and relegated to maintenance of the way use. It has since been removed. (Photograph by Eldon Neff.)

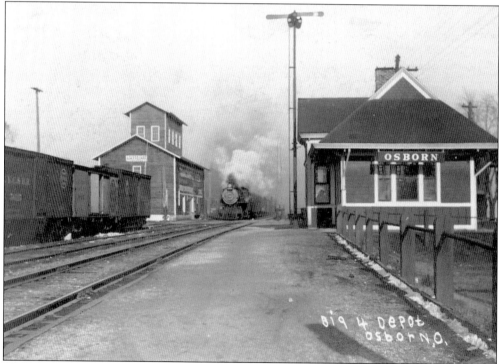

This Osborn combination depot was built to standard plans of the Cleveland, Cincinnati, Chicago, and St. Louis Railroad, probably in the 1890s. It was first erected on the far side of the Big Four track. To the left in this c. 1907 view were the Erie tracks and their station site. (Author's collection.)

Two

NEW YORK
CENTRAL LINES

The Mad River and Lake Erie Railroad finally entered Springfield in 1848, providing the first Ohio connection between Lake Erie (Sandusky) and the Ohio River and joining the Little Miami Railroad, which had entered Springfield two years before. In 1872, Springfield was connected to Cincinnati by the opening of the Cincinnati and Springfield Railroad, also commonly called the "Short Line." The new line almost immediately was leased to the Cleveland, Columbus, Cincinnati, and Indianapolis (CCC&I) Railroad, commonly known as the "Bee Line." Between Dayton and Hamilton, this line more or less paralleled the CH&D Railroad—the CH&D on the west side of the Great Miami River and the CCC&I on the east.

The second line to build into the western part of Cincinnati was the Cincinnati and Indiana Railroad. The line made use of the old towpath of the Whitewater Canal and began operations by 1863. After a couple of name changes, the line became part of the Cincinnati, Indianapolis, St. Louis, and Chicago Railroad in 1866. The surviving lines became part of the Cleveland, Cincinnati, Chicago, and St. Louis Railroad (CCC&StL), the Big Four, in 1889. The Big Four came under New York Central Railroad control in 1930. The Norfolk Southern became the operator in 1998.

The Cincinnati, Van Wert, and Michigan (CVW&M) completed a line from Addison Junction, Michigan, to Franklin on the CCC&I in the late 1880s. In 1897, the Cincinnati Northern (CN) Railroad formed to assume control of the Ohio part of the Cincinnati, Jackson, and Mackinaw (CJ&M) Railway, a renamed and extended version of the CVW&M. This is not to be confused with the narrow-gauge Cincinnati Northern Railway that opened in 1881 between Norwood and Lebanon and became, in 1885, the Cincinnati, Lebanon, and Northern (CL&N) Railway, a later Pennsylvania Railroad property. By 1902, the Cincinnati Northern Railroad was under Big Four (New York Central) control.

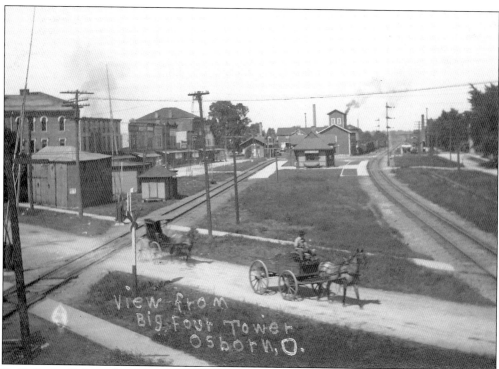

By 1912, the Osborn depot had been moved across the Big Four track and been altered with an addition and second vestibule so that it could serve as a joint depot for the Big Four and Erie Railroads. The earlier Erie depot is just beyond the relocated Big Four depot. Close examination of this card shows a Big Four water tank behind the feed mill and an elevated watchman's tower. This view was taken from the Big Four interlocking tower where the Erie and Big Four crossed. In 1921, as part of the Huffman Dam project, the Big Four depot was relocated for the second time to the new alignment. This view, shot in 1940, shows the depot and in the distance, Fairborn tower. (Above, author's collection; below, photograph by Eldon Neff.)

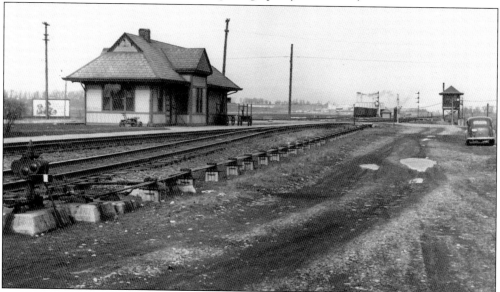

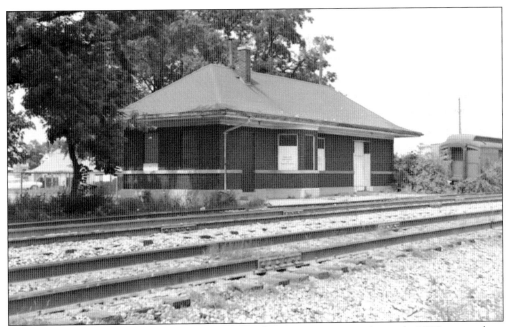

West Carrollton received a brick replacement depot sometime in the early 1900s to replace an earlier frame depot. The depot was still there in the late 1970s, but unused and boarded. (Photograph by the author.)

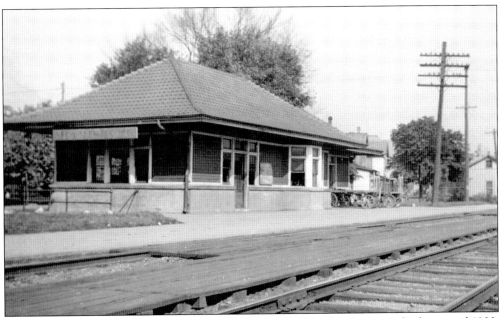

It is in between trains at Miamisburg in the mid-1900s. When this depot was built, around 1900, the former frame combination depot was converted to freight use. This passenger depot also contained a basement storage area. It remains in business use. (David P. Oroszi collection.)

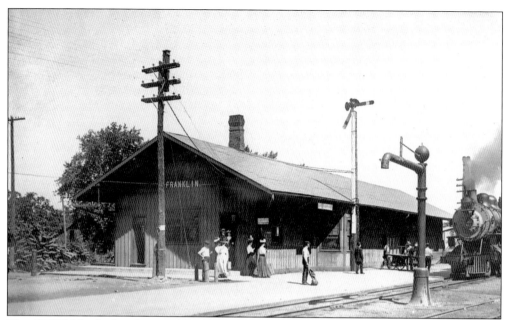

The CCC&I built this depot at Fourth Street in Franklin in 1872. It has segregated waiting rooms—one for women and children, and the other for men. The iron column is a standpipe for watering the steam engines. This depot was on the old line on the east side of the Great Miami River. In 1911, in a move to shorten the line, a cutoff was built on the west side of the river through the Carlisle area. (Author's collection.)

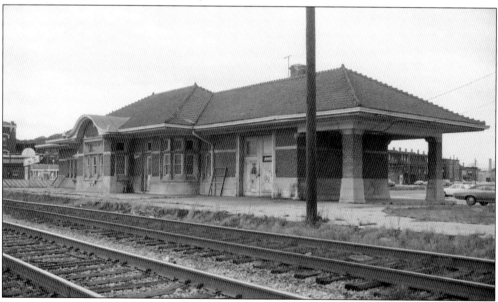

The CCC&I opened a frame combination depot in 1872 at Central Avenue and Charles Street in Middletown. A horse-car line provided a connection to the CH&D depot in West Middletown beginning in 1879. The depot burned to the ground March 12, 1884. Another depot was built on the same site and was used until 1909 when the depot pictured here opened. A separate freight house was built on Manchester Avenue. In 1938, eighteen New York Central (NYC) passenger trains used this depot daily. The NYC closed this depot in 1961. It is now in business use. (Author's collection.)

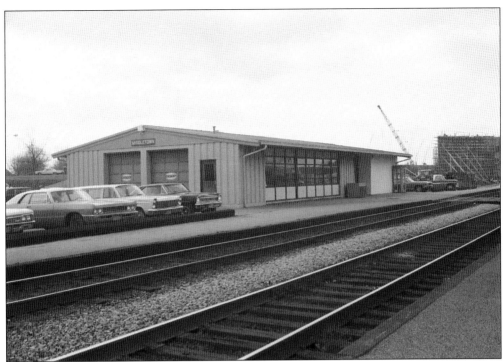

The New York Central built this modern replacement passenger depot in 1961. It sat directly across the tracks from the 1909 depot. It was not used many years, for passenger service to Middletown was discontinued April 30, 1971. (Photograph by Charles Garvin.)

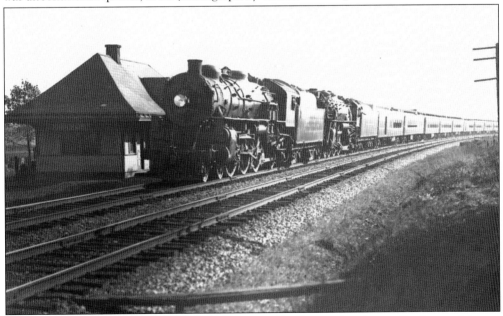

The Cleveland, Cincinnati, Chicago, and St. Louis, or Big Four, replaced an earlier depot at Monroe with this structure in the early 1900s. The design has a decided New York Central influence. In this view from 1931, New York Central's *Ohio State Limited* heads east past the depot. (Dan E. Finfrock collection.)

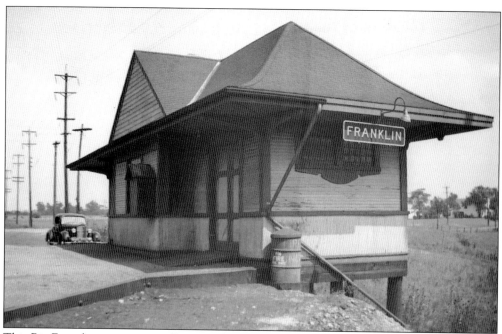

This Big Four depot was originally erected at Kyles, but reportedly in January 1941 was loaded on a flatcar and moved to the CN crossing on Lower Carlisle Road near Carlisle Junction. It served as the Franklin depot on the cut-off. The old Big Four depot had been across the river in downtown Franklin before the realignment. (David P. Oroszi collection.)

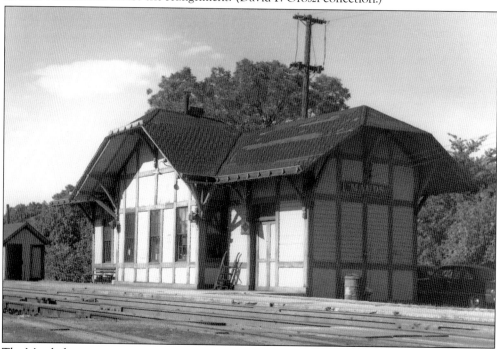

The Mauds depot is an example of another standard plan CCC&StL depot. This plan was repeated across the system. The half-hipped roof and wide overhang made this a distinct structure. In this August 1950 view, the depot was still well maintained. (Cincinnati Railroad Club collection.)

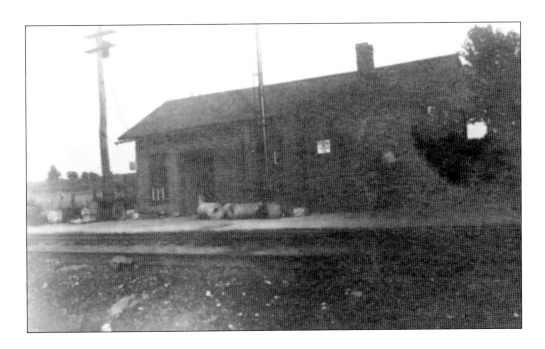

Above is an earlier depot from West Chester, probably dating to the 1870s when the CCC&I connected Dayton and Cincinnati. In 1912, the below combination depot replaced this earlier structure. Further south, the CCC&I had a frame depot at Lockland. It burned to the ground in 1971. A Big Four depot once serving Elmwood Place was relocated in the 1960s to a business in Carthage in the 1960s. (Above, author's collection; below, Dan E. Finfrock collection.)

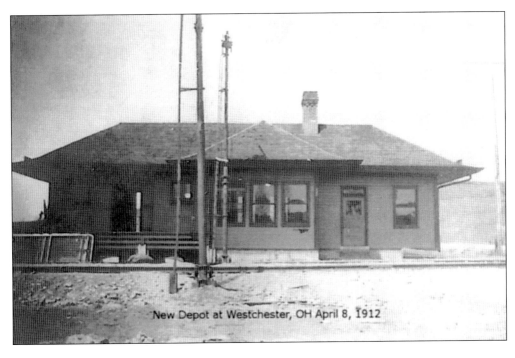

New Depot at Westchester, OH April 8, 1912

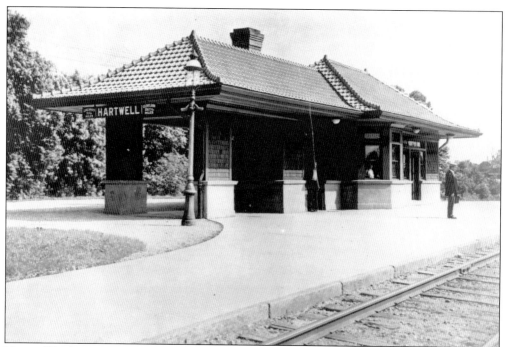

Hartwell had two impressive commuter depots. This was the passenger depot of the CCC&StL. Nearby was a frame depot on the CH&D, with second-floor living space for the agent. Both have long since disappeared. (Author's collection.)

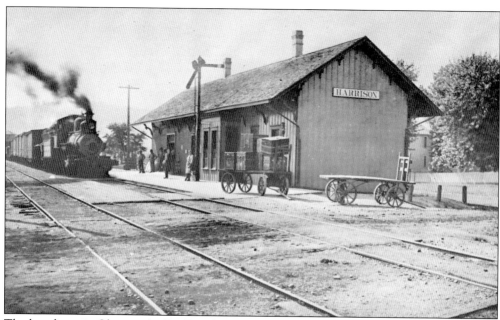

The last depot in Ohio on the Big Four line, up the Whitewater River Valley, was at Harrison. This view shows the Big Four depot on Railroad Avenue and an incoming passenger train around 1907. (Author's collection.)

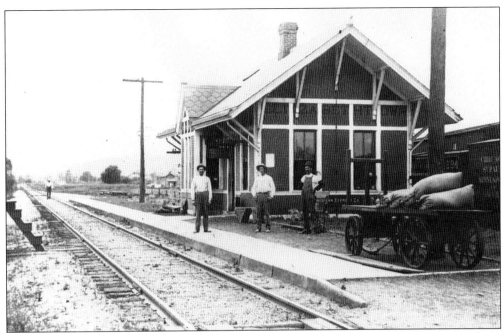

The CCC&StL line along the Ohio River directly parallels the old Ohio and Mississippi Railway, later the B&OSW line, as it heads to St. Louis. This is the earlier depot at Elizabethtown in the 1890s. It lasted until the line was double-tracked. (W. Steigerwald collection.)

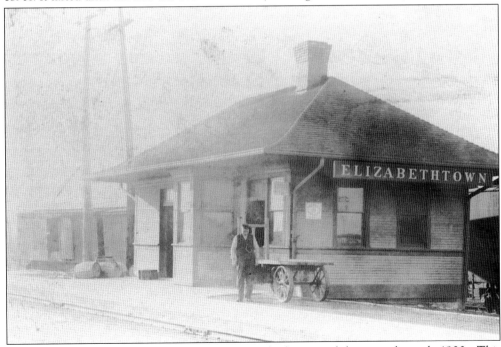

Elizabethtown's station agent proudly poses outside the second depot in the early 1900s. This depot was built to one of many Big Four Railroad depot floorplans. Just the simple curve of the eaves makes it a pleasing structure. Unfortunately the depot was demolished in a 1917 train wreck. (Author's collection.)

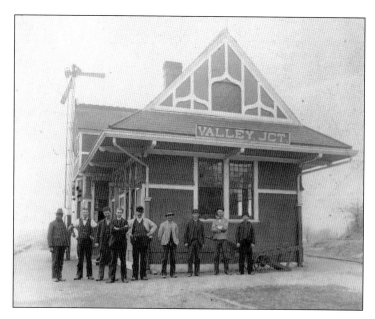

At Valley Junction, the Big Four split; one line following the Whitewater River Valley and the other heading down the Ohio River Valley. This junction depot, photographed in 1895, was torn down in 1930. (W. Steigerwald collection.)

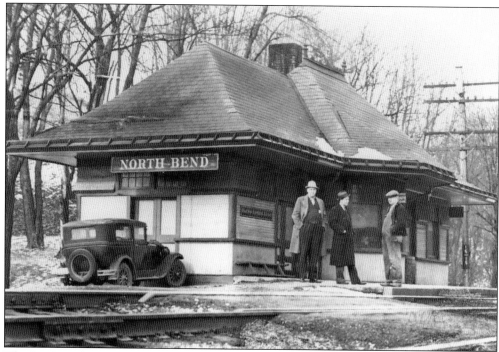

The Big Four located depots at North Bend (above) and Cleves (next page), although the communities were only a few miles apart. The depots were built to a similar plan. Well-dressed railroad officials are conferring with a worker on the platform of the North Bend depot around 1940. (Cincinnati Railroad Club collection.)

46

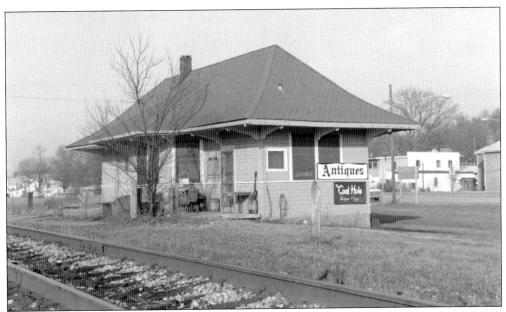

The Cleves depot became an antique shop after it closed. This view was taken in December 1973. In later years, it was apparently torn down by a new owner and a replica built to house a new business. (Photograph by author.)

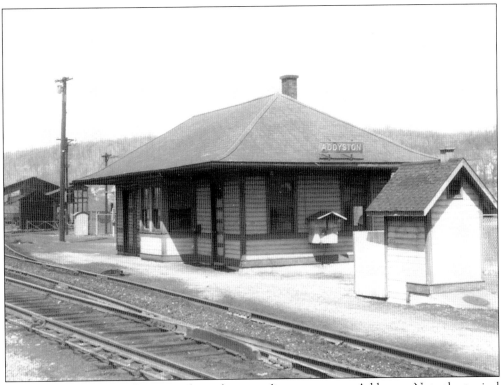

This appears to be a replacement depot for an earlier structure at Addyston. Note the typical cast-iron town board in this 1960 photograph. (Otis Flinchpaugh collection.)

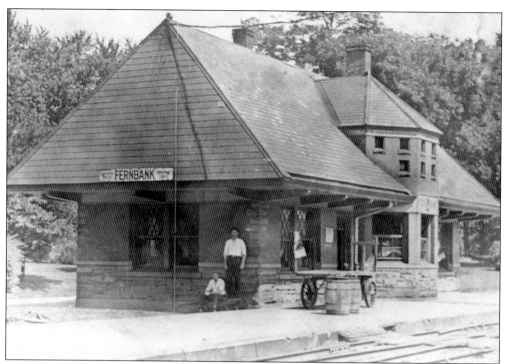

Fernbank's CCC&StL depot was a busy commuter station on the Big Four. The line erected a number of unique depots along this stretch to serve the growing suburban population of greater Cincinnati. Several appear to have been designed with community input and the use of outside architects, rather than the engineering office of the CCC&StL. (W. Steigerwald collection.)

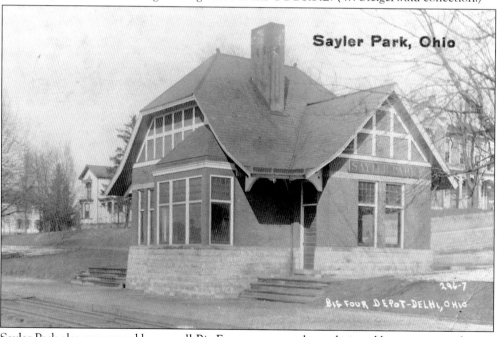

Sayler Park also was served by a small Big Four commuter depot designed by a private architect, perhaps commissioned by a neighborhood organization. (Gary D. Rolih collection.)

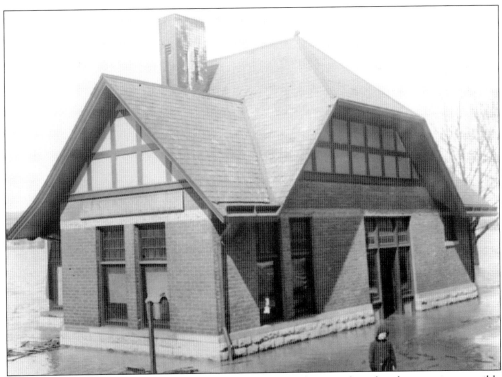

The problem with many of the depots along these river lines is that they became inaccessible during floods. The 1913 flood wreaked havoc along many of the railroads of Southwest Ohio. Sayler Park was no exception. (W. Steigerwald collection.)

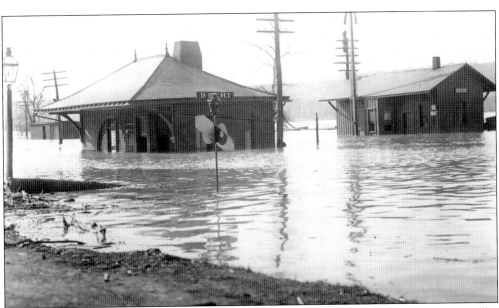

In March 1913, both the Big Four (in the foreground) and B&OSW depots were unusable in Delhi. Maintenance crews quickly cleaned them of flood debris, and repairs were made shortly after the waters receded. The depots returned to service quickly. (W. Steigerwald collection.)

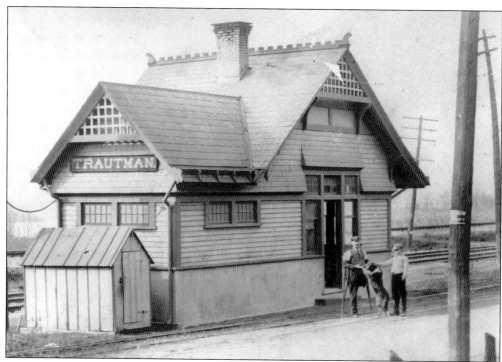

Samuel John Hissett stands outside the Trautman CCC&StL depot around 1910. Hissett lost a leg in a rail mishap and spent the rest of his railroad career as the agent at this commuter station. Nearby, a Catholic boarding school, which became the College of Mount St. Joseph in 1920, opened on the hilltop overlooking the Ohio River in 1906. Neeb Road once ran down a terraced hillside planted with grape vines to this passenger depot near the river. This depot served many of the "Mount's" students, staff, and professors in the early 1900s. Closer to Cincinnati was a depot at Sedamsville. (Above, W. Steigerwald collection; below, author's collection.)

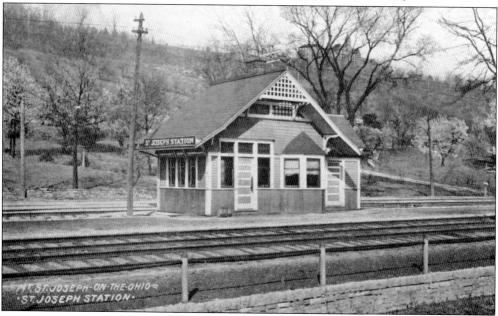

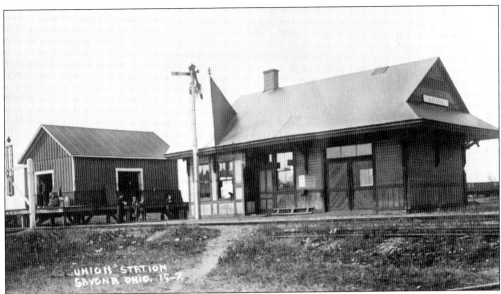

At Savona, the Cincinnati, Jackson, and Mackinaw Railroad (CJ&M) crossed the Big Four Troy Branch. Rails reached here in 1884. This was one of two towered depots built by the line; the other one was constructed at Addison Junction in Michigan. Savona was a joint agency serving passengers of each road. This depot and the one at the next station to the south, Castine, has been gone for many years. (David P. Oroszi collection.)

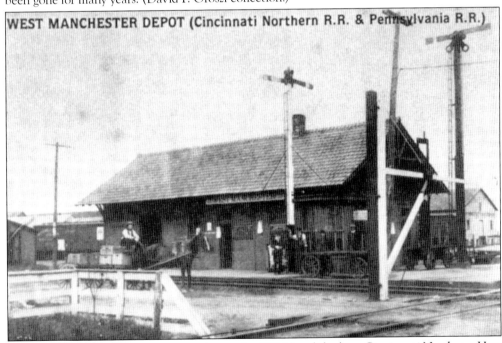

West Manchester was an important point on the CJ&M and the later Cincinnati Northern. Here the line crossed the former Dayton and Western line of the Pennsylvania Railroad, reaching town in 1885. The CJ&M built this depot north of the diamond, joining an already present Pittsburg, Cincinnati, Chicago, and St. Louis depot. At this time, an interlocking tower of PCC&StL design was erected at the new crossing. By the 1970s, only the tower remained. (David P. Oroszi collection.)

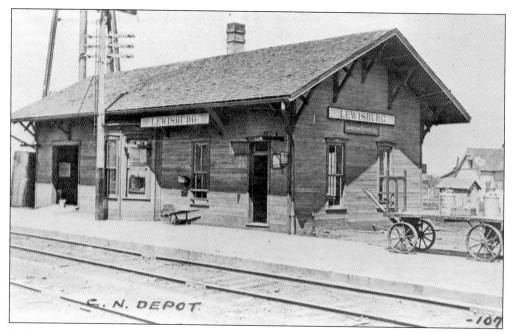

Rails reached Lewisburg in 1885. The above c. 1910 postcard view shows a well-kept depot platform, although the depot appears in need of a coat of paint. After closing in 1981, this depot was moved to land near the I-70 interchange, where it sat unused for many years. Luckily it was saved by the local historical society in 1992 and moved to the town park, where it now serves as a museum. Rails reached West Alexandria in 1886. The CJ&M built a number of combination depots in the style seen below along their line, another one being further south at Germantown. The Dayton and Western Traction line crossed the CN in the foreground in the early 1900s. The depot remains as a residence. (Both, author's collection.)

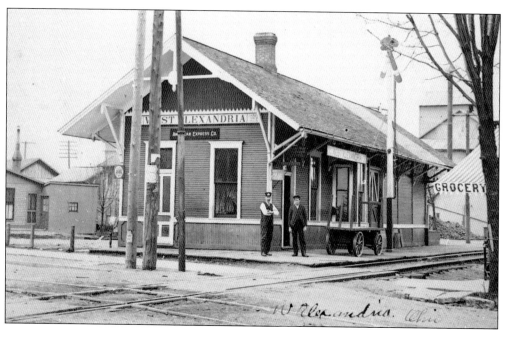

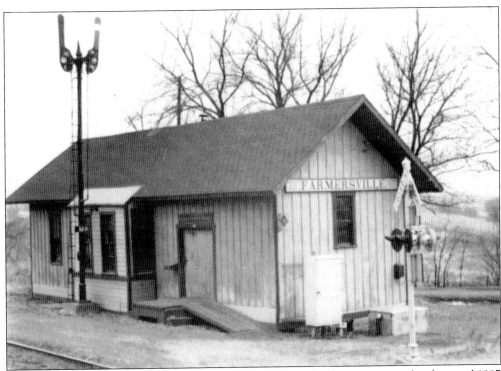

Farmersville's 1887 CJ&M depot remains in business use. The depot was revitalized around 1997 after sitting vacant for years. Unfortunately the CJ&M depot at Ingomar, the next station north, was torn down long ago. (Dan E. Finfrock collection.)

Rails were laid into Germantown in 1887, and the CJ&M appears to have converted an existing building into the town's first depot. This structure served the line for about five years. (Dan E. Finfrock collection.)

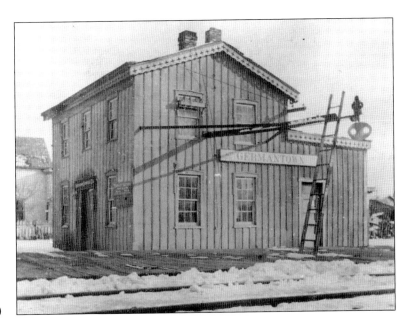

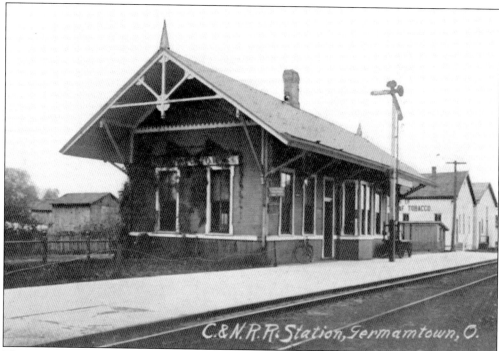

This c. 1910 postal view of the 1892 CJ&M combination depot at Germantown shows the ornate use of finials and bargeboards in the original design of CJ&M depots. These were later commonly removed by maintenance crews to reduce the cost of depot upkeep. At some point, the CN added a separate freight station. The Germantown depot has been restored and sits in the town park. (Author's collection.)

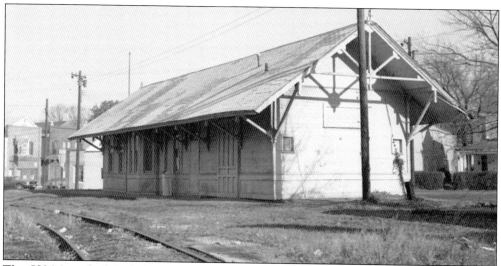

The CJ&M reached Carlisle in 1887 and built into Franklin in 1888. The CJ&M had a joint agency with the CH&D at Carlisle. Franklin's Cincinnati Northern depot, at the corner of Sixth and Main Streets, dates to 1888. By 1911, after completion of the Big Four's Carlisle cutoff, some 20 passenger trains called at the depot daily. CN passenger service came to an end February 3, 1938. The last Big Four passenger train called April 28, 1951. This view was recorded in November 1973. The depot was restored in 1995. (Photograph by the author.)

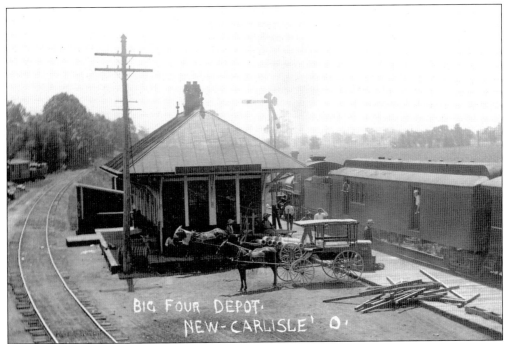

Rails of the Indiana, Bloomington, and Western Railroad reached New Carlisle in the early 1880s. This line became part of the CCC&StL in 1889. An omnibus awaits passengers needing a lift to the local hotel in the above c. 1907 scene. Another wagon has some items to be loaded on the baggage and express car. By 1949, the depot, now under New York Central influence, had received a new roof and paint scheme. The last passenger train stopped around 1950. The depot is no longer extant. (Above, author's collection; below, photograph by Eldon Neff.)

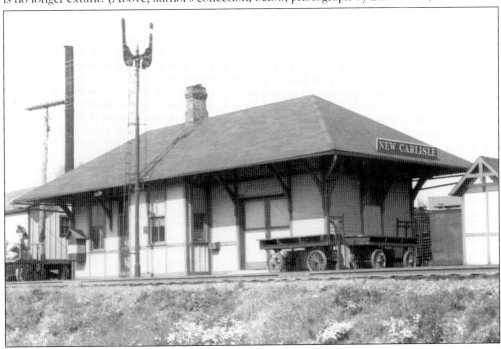

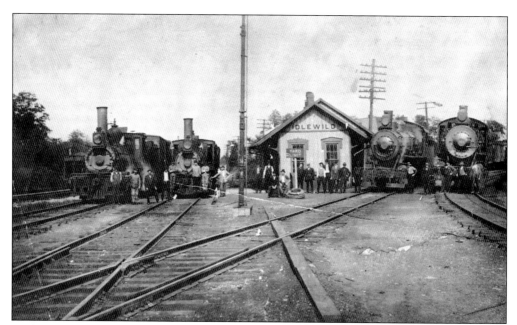

In this obviously posed c. 1910 westerly view (above) of the junction at Idlewild, two CL&N locomotives are to the left of the depot, and two N&W locomotives are on the right. All the train crews and depot staff, plus anyone else that happened to be around, line up for the photographer. The location is now west of Montgomery Road, near the boundary of Evansville and Avondale. The below view is from the 1920s. This depot was built around 1901. (Both, N&W Historical Photograph Collection, Virginia Tech University Library.)

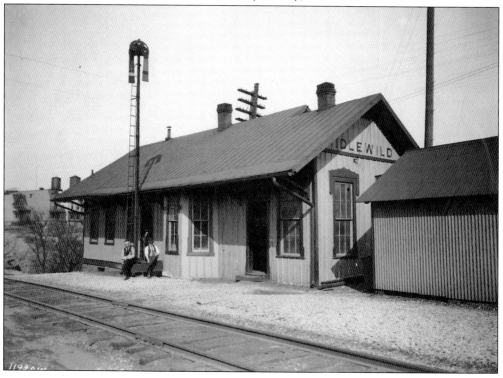

Three

NORFOLK AND WESTERN LINES

The Cincinnati and Eastern (C&E) Railway, which started as the Cincinnati, Batavia, and Williamsburg was organized in 1876 to build a 3-foot narrow-gauge line from Cincinnati to Portsmouth. The C&E began tracklaying in 1876 at Batavia Junction (later Clare) on the Little Miami Railroad. From Batavia Junction, the company built to Idlewild for a planned junction with the narrow-gauge Miami Valley Railroad, but the Miami Valley never reached the tracklaying stage. The connection was finally made in 1881, when the Cincinnati Northern Railway opened between Norwood and Lebanon. Financial problems led to reorganization as the Cincinnati, Portsmouth, and Eastern in 1879. The C&E opened a short-lived branch to New Richmond on the Ohio River in 1880. After linking Cincinnati and Portsmouth in August 1884, a connection was made with the Norfolk and Western Railway at the C&E's eastern end. The line became nicknamed the "Peavine" because of its twisting route through the bedrock hills of southern Ohio. In an unusual move, the C&E was converted to standard gauge between Winchester and Portsmouth in May 1885, and then returned to narrow gauge by a later receiver several months after. Financial problems continued, and the line was reorganized in 1886 as the Ohio and Northwestern Railroad. The O&NW ended the narrow-gauge days of the line in November 1887. The branch to New Richmond was sold in 1887 and became the Cincinnati, New Richmond, and Ohio River Railroad, only to be abandoned by the 1890s. Financial problems continued and led to a reorganization of the O&NW as the Cincinnati, Portsmouth, and Virginia (CP&V) Railroad in 1891. Just before 1900, the CP&V established a connection between Idlewild, and the B&O (ex-Marietta and Cincinnati) at Bond Hill, and the CH&D at Ivorydale. The Norfolk and Western (N&W) Railway took over the CP&V in 1901, making it the Cincinnati-Portsmouth segment. The N&W merged with the Southern Railway in 1982 to become the Norfolk Southern Corporation.

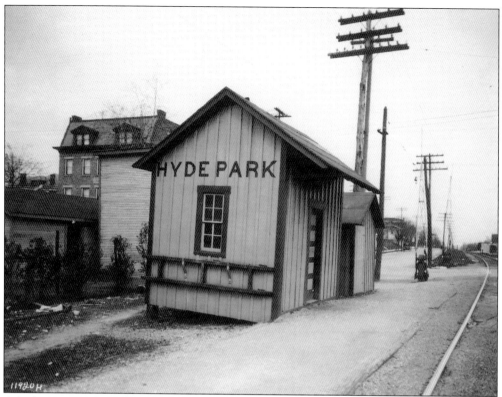

A little over a mile to the east of Idlewild was this passenger shelter at Hyde Park. Unmanned shelters like this were used along commuter routes, where the depots were closely spaced, and at country stops where passenger patronage was low. (N&W Historical Photograph Collection, Virginia Tech University Library.)

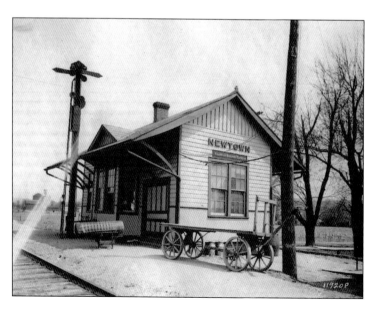

After crossing the Little Miami Railroad and Little Miami River, the Cincinnati and Eastern reached Newtown in the late 1870s. The N&W built this depot at Newtown around 1901. (N&W Historical Photograph Collection, Virginia Tech University Library.)

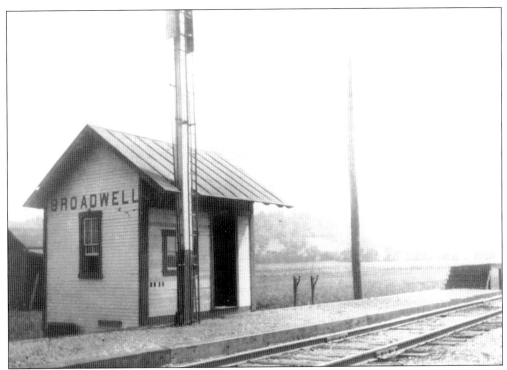

The above early-1900s view shows the small depot at Broadwell. Note the old-style order board. Around 1917, the station name was changed to Ancor. Look closely and the notch in the roofline where the order board once was located can be seen. The name was changed because of confusion with another railroad station called Broadwell in Athens County. (Above, Gary D. Rolih collection; below, N&W Historical Photograph Collection, Virginia Tech University Library.)

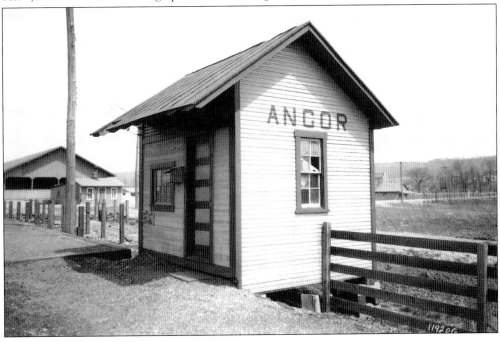

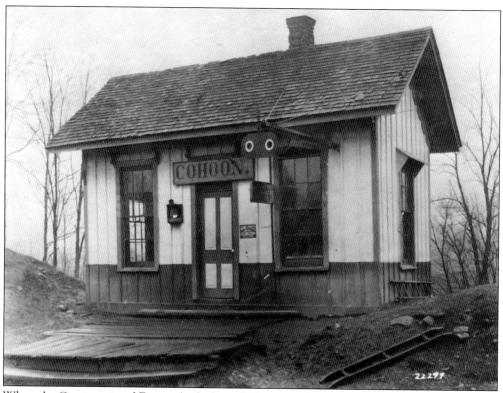

When the Cincinnati and Eastern built through this part of Hamilton County they established a station at Cohoon. The above view was taken in spring 1875. By the 1920s, the name of the town was changed to Perintown. Only the section house, shown behind the Perintown depot (below), remains standing. (Both, N&W Historical Photograph Collection, Virginia Tech University Library.)

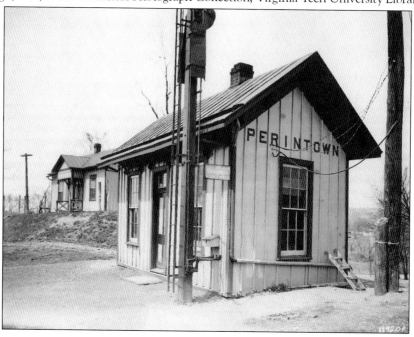

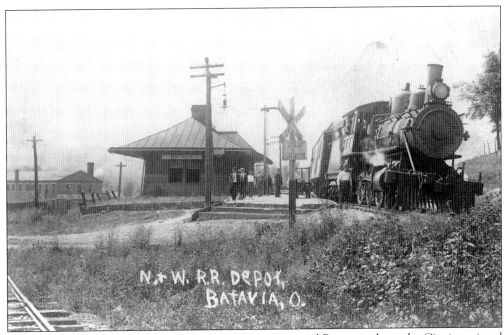

Batavia was the largest community between Cincinnati and Portsmouth on the Cincinnati and Eastern line. The C&E began to serve Batavia in 1877. This brick and stone depot located between Clough Pike and Main Street was the most impressive on the line. The last passenger train left here in April 1971. Unfortunately it was demolished in January 1989. (Author's collection.)

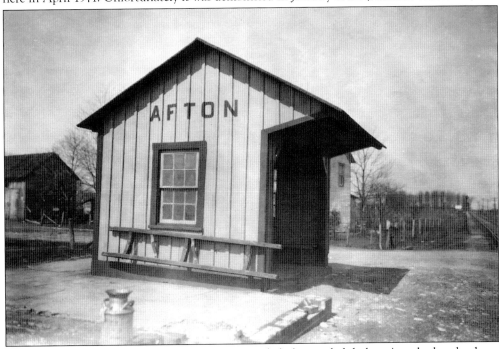

Afton's depot, shown in the 1920s, was an unattended, three-sided shelter. Attached to the depot is a barrel skid for loading freight cars. The milk can was destined for a nearby creamery. (N&W Historical Photograph Collection, Virginia Tech University Library.)

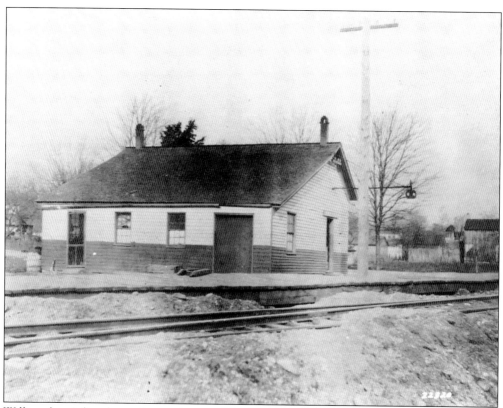

Williamsburg's first depot, shown above on March 28, 1896, was probably built by the Cincinnati, Portsmouth, and Virginia Railroad (CP&V). The second depot in Williamsburg was probably constructed around 1901 when the N&W took over the CP&V. (Both, N&W Historical Photograph Collection, Virginia Tech University Library.)

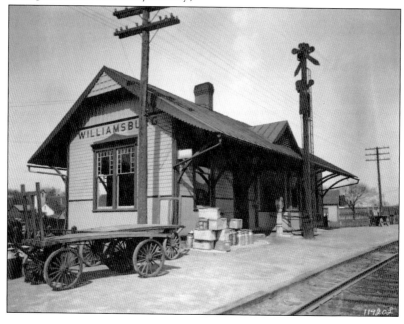

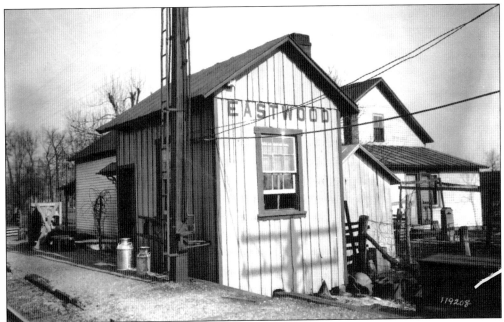

East of Williamsburg was this small depot at Eastwood, photographed in the early 1920s. Note the old-style order board and milk cans awaiting pick-up. (N&W Historical Photograph Collection, Virginia Tech University Library.)

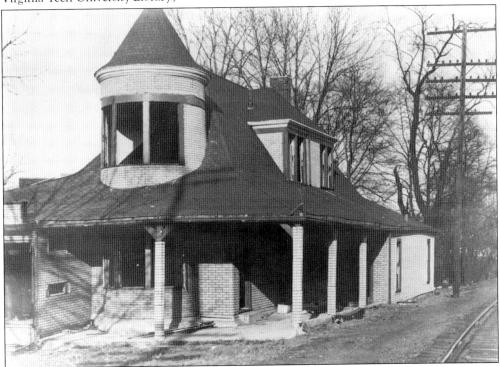

Around 1900, the N&W built a connector from Idlewild north to the B&OSW at Bond Hill and the CH&D at Ivorydale. This view shows the Bond Hill passenger depot nearing completion. (Dan E. Finfrock collection.)

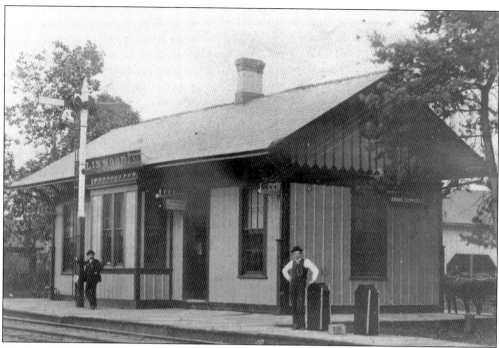

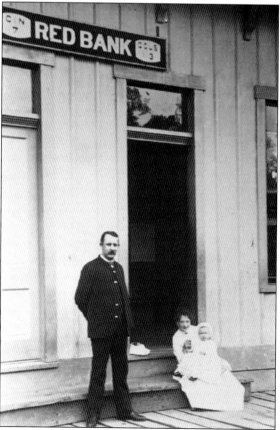

The Little Miami Railroad maintained the above depot at Linwood, the station for Mount Washington. In this c. 1897 view, the surroundings were still pastoral. By 1937, the depot had been relegated to storage use at the east throat to Undercliff yard. On the Ohio River floodplain, the depot was inundated by floodwaters a number of times. At left is a close-up view of the Little Miami depot at Red Bank. The agent and family pose on a pleasant day. (Above, Cincinnati Railroad Club collection; left, author's collection.)

Four

PENNSYLVANIA LINES

Construction began in the late 1830s at Cincinnati and Xenia on the first line in Southwest Ohio—the Little Miami Railroad. The Columbus and Xenia Railroad opened between the namesakes in 1850 and soon became favored over the original Little Miami route into Springfield. The Eaton and Hamilton Railroad formed in 1847 to build the Ohio portion of a line between Richmond, Indiana, and Hamilton. As the Cincinnati, Richmond, and Chicago (CR&C) Railroad, the line was extended to Rendcomb Junction in 1888. The Cincinnati, Wilmington, and Zanesville Railroad, joined the Little Miami at Morrow in 1856; it became the Cincinnati and Muskingum Valley Railroad in 1898.

The Dayton and Western Railroad opened from Dayton to New Paris in 1853. The Dayton, Xenia, and Belpre Railroad completed a route from Dayton to Xenia in 1858. In 1888, the Cincinnati and Richmond Railroad opened between Red Bank and Hamilton. In 1890–1892, the Middletown and Cincinnati Railway linked Middletown and Kings Mills. By 1890, these lines were part of the Pittsburgh, Cincinnati, Chicago, and St. Louis Railway and in the 1920s part of the Pennsylvania Railroad.

Lebanon received its railroad connection in the 1870s with the start of construction of the narrow-gauge Miami Valley Railway. Financial problems prevented completion of this line. The project was revived in 1880, when the Toledo, Delphos, and Burlington Railroad acquired the Miami Valley roadbed. A new company was formed—the Cincinnati Northern Railway—to complete the line into Cincinnati and to a station at Dodds, 6 miles north of Lebanon. Trains were running between Norwood and Dodds by 1881 and into Cincinnati by early 1882. The Cincinnati Northern became another link in the Toledo, Delphos, and Burlington narrow-gauge empire when it was connected with the new TD&B line, between Dodds and Lebanon Junction (Shakertown) on the Dayton and Southeastern. Financial problems accrued. The stretch between Dodds and Cincinnati became the Cincinnati, Lebanon, and Northern (CL&N) Railway. In 1893, the Dayton, Lebanon, and Cincinnati Railroad began operating the portion between Dodds and Lebanon Junction, after converting it to standard gauge. The CL&N, converted to standard gauge in 1894, came under Pennsylvania control in 1896.

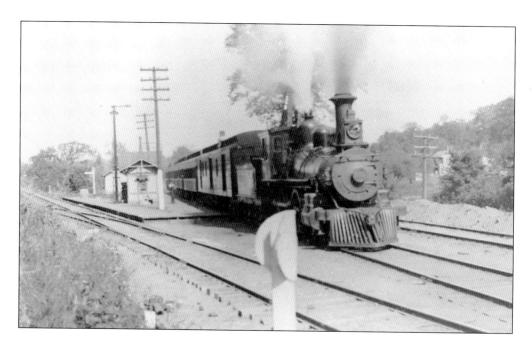

Here are two early 1900 views of the 1890s depot at Red Bank's Rendcomb Junction, where the PCC&StL's Richmond branch begins. Above, a Little Miami westbound train passes the facilities on its way to Pearl Street Station in downtown Cincinnati. The view below shows a westbound train on the Cincinnati and Richmond line. A frame-interlocking tower was located just west of the depot. In later years, the depot was gone, and a newer brick tower guarded the junction. (Both, Dan E. Finfrock collection.)

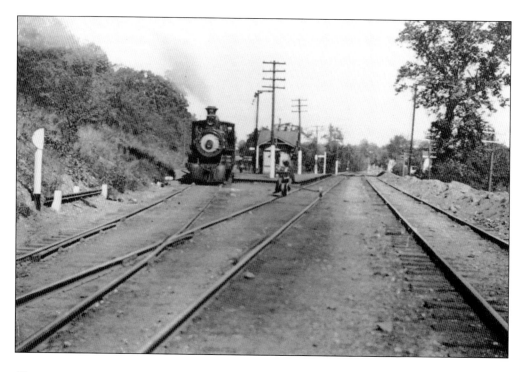

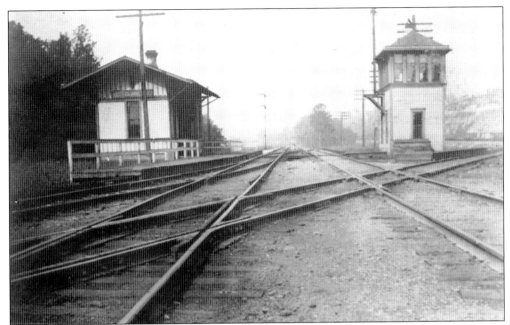

The junction of the C&E and Little Miami, originally called Batavia Junction, became Clare in 1903. The crossing was protected by Clare tower, and passengers from the PRR and N&W were accommodated at this standard plan PCC&StL combination depot in the early 1900s. The early-1900 view shows the depot after it had been moved from its original location diagonally across the diamond in 1898. A train derailment in 1921 led to replacement of the wooden tower with a brick one in 1924. (N&W Historical Photograph Collection, Virginia Tech University Library.)

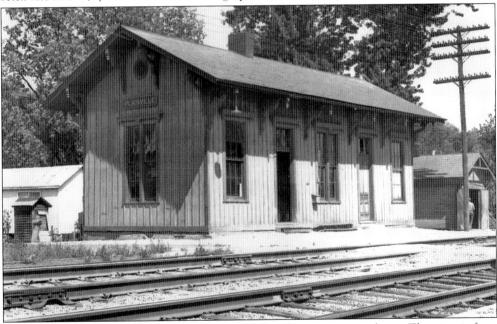

Plainville residents boarded the Little Miami at this frame passenger depot. The view is from August 14, 1937. The circular window in the gable was an architectural element appearing in many early Little Miami Railroad buildings. (Cincinnati Railroad Club collection.)

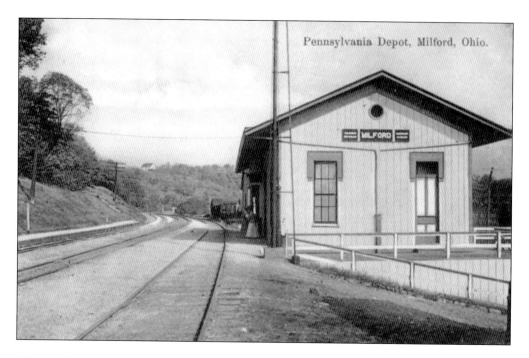

Along with Morrow, the Milford depot is among the oldest still extant depots in the Midwest. The above c. 1910 postcard view shows a couple of passengers waiting for the next Cincinnati-bound train. Below is the modified Milford depot on October 27, 1940, in Pennsylvania Railroad colors. A portion of the building dates to 1843. (Above, Gary D. Rolih collection; below, Cincinnati Railroad Club collection.)

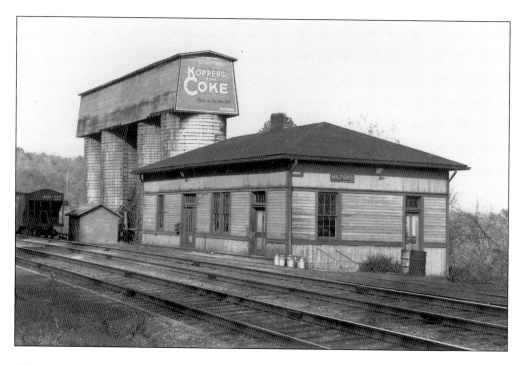

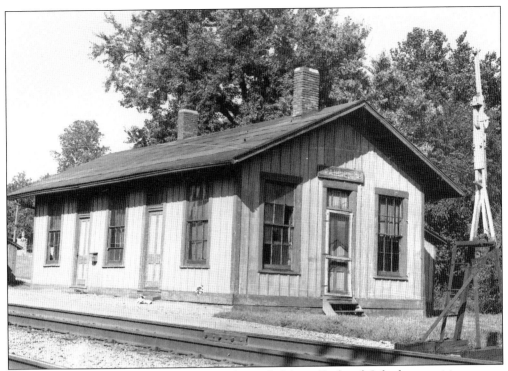

Branch Hill depot was built to a design of the Little Miami Railroad. It had two waiting rooms, but the station agent's office lacked a bay window. This shot is from August 1937. (Cincinnati Railroad Club collection.)

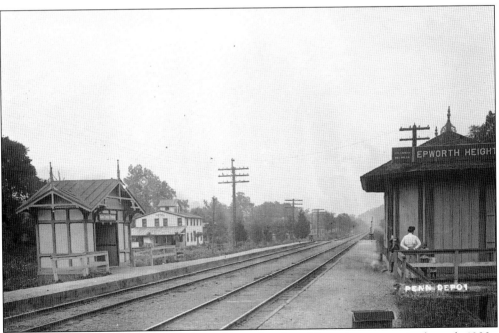

Epworth Heights had facilities for both northbound and southbound passengers in the early 1900s. Commuters made heavy use of this small depot. (Gary D. Rolih collection.)

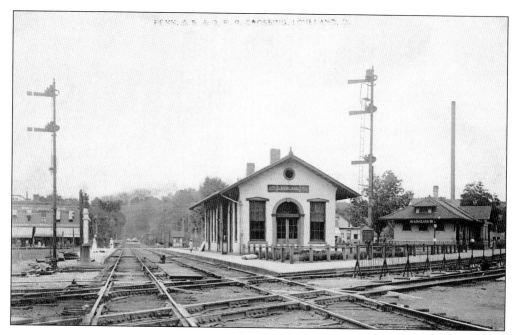

Loveland was served by this brick Pittsburgh, Cincinnati, and St. Louis passenger depot at the diamond with the B&O, pictured above on August 28, 1937. The depot probably dates to around 1870 and replaces an earlier Little Miami frame depot. To the left across the tracks, a frame standard design PRR interlocking tower, dating to around 1912, guarded the crossing. To the right is the B&O passenger depot. Southeast of the diamond was a park area near a railroad water tank and turntable. By the early 1970s, the Pennsylvania (PRR) Railroad depot was long gone; the tower remained, although sided. The PRR, former Little Miami, tracks were torn out in the late 1970s. (Above, Cincinnati Railroad Club collection; below, Gary D. Rolih collection.)

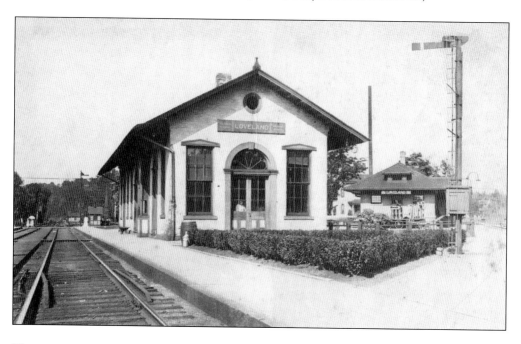

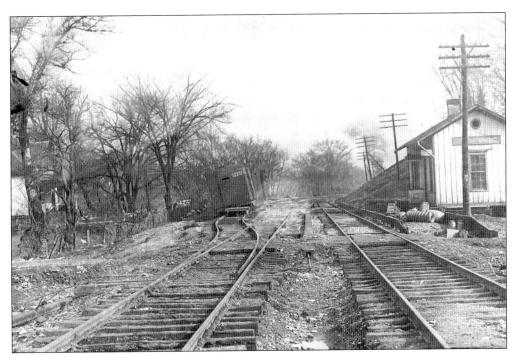

The Little Miami's tracks at Fosters were underwater during the 1913 flood, but the depot was not permanently damaged. The above view was taken shortly after the waters receded. Below, the Morrow accommodation pauses at the depot for a few passengers as workers cleaning out the depot take a break. The depot at Fosters was probably originally similar to the Plainville depot. The bay window appears to have been added later. (Above, author's collection; below, Cincinnati Railroad Club collection.)

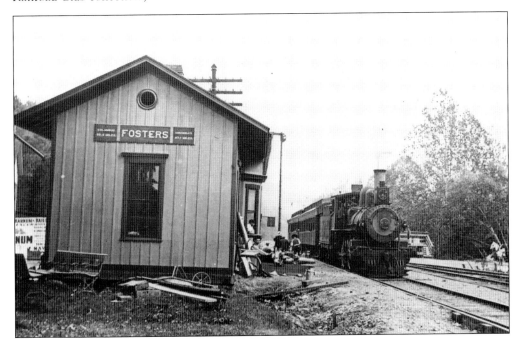

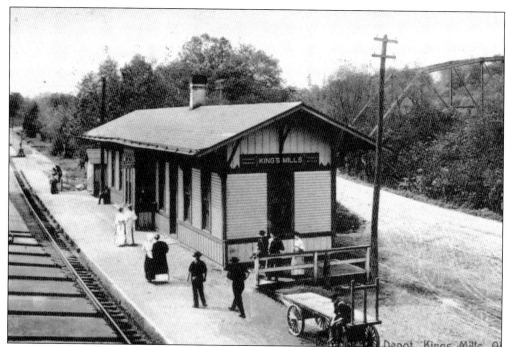

Kings Mills appears to be a later design, probably erected by the PCC&StL in the late 1880s. Many depots of similar design once dotted the entire PCC&StL system. Above, passengers and staff mill about, waiting for the next passenger train. Kings Mills was still an active agency when photographed below on May 1, 1949. (Above, author's collection; below, Cincinnati Railroad Club collection.)

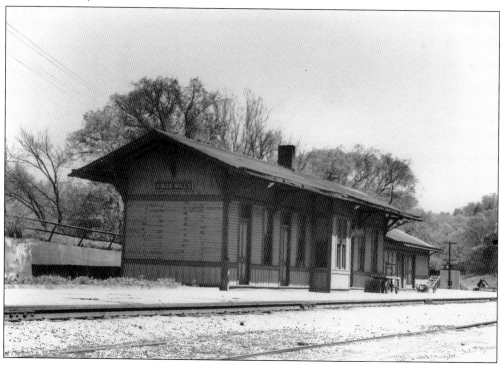

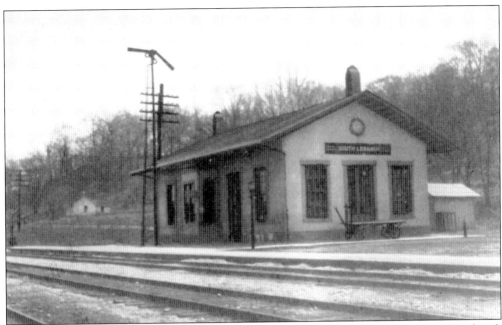

South Lebanon appears to be built to an early set of structure plans of the Little Miami Railroad. As with Fosters, the bay window may have been a later addition. (Author's collection.)

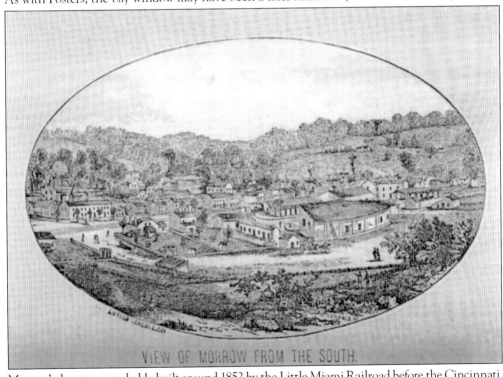

VIEW OF MORROW FROM THE SOUTH.

Morrow's depot was probably built around 1852 by the Little Miami Railroad before the Cincinnati, Wilmington, and Zanesville arrived in town. It ranks as one of the oldest still-extant depots in Ohio. This sketch is from the 1854 *Ohio Railway Guide* and shows the depot with an arriving passenger train in the center. A roundhouse is adjacent. (Author's collection.)

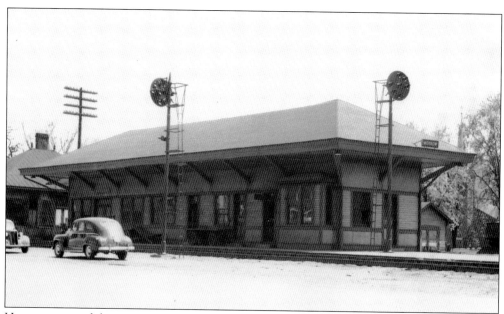

Here is a view of the Morrow depot in the early 1940s. The depot has since been restored and now serves cyclists traveling the Greater Miami Trail. It ranks among the oldest depots in the Midwest. (Cincinnati Railroad Club collection.)

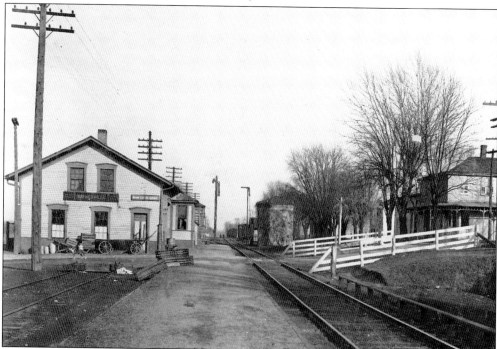

Waynesville was located on the west side of the Little Miami River; its depot on the Little Miami was on the east bank at a location called Corwin. This c. 1907 view shows the depot, a PCC&StL wooden water tank just behind the depot, and a PCC&StL train order office just behind the concrete water tank on the right dating to the early days of the Little Miami Railroad. The building to the right was a boardinghouse. (Author's collection.)

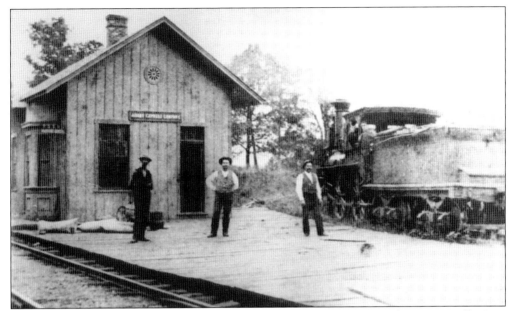

Just north of Waynesville was the depot at Claysville Junction, where the Waynesville, Port William, and Jeffersonville Railroad joined the Little Miami. This narrow-gauge line extended from here some 23 miles to Allenville on the Dayton and Southeastern. After reorganization and converting to standard gauge, the track was torn up in 1887. (Richard A. Lenehan collection.)

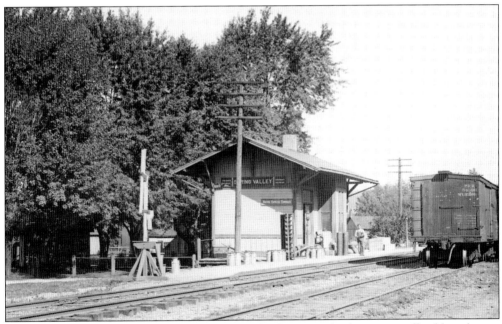

Spring Valley was the first station south of Xenia. The depot was the destination of health-seekers in the late 1800s. Horse-drawn carriages and wagons brought passengers to nearby Magnetic Springs. This depot probably dates to the 1880s and is of PC&StL design. (Gary D. Rolih collection.)

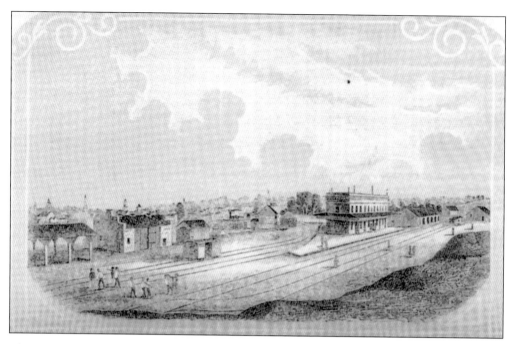

The Little Miami Railroad entered Xenia in 1845, and for the first few years apparently used a Detroit Street building as their depot. After the Columbus and Xenia Railroad connected the namesakes in 1850, this large two-story depot and office building was erected at the junction. The above view is a sketch from the 1854 *Ohio Railway Guide*. The track to the left of the depot is the Little Miami to Springfield; the track to the right is the Columbus and Xenia. Beyond the depot is a freight house. By the 1870s, Xenia was a railroad center. Around 1880, a two-story brick building (below) was constructed where the old freight house had stood to house a telegraph office and express and baggage facilities. A new freight house was constructed across the track. (Both, author's collection.)

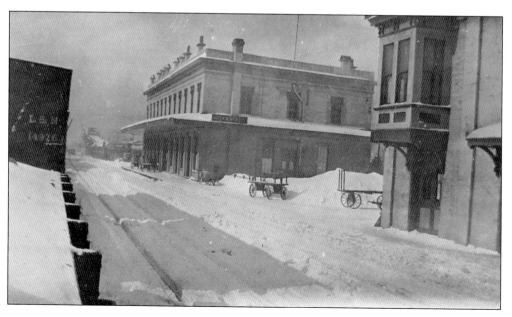

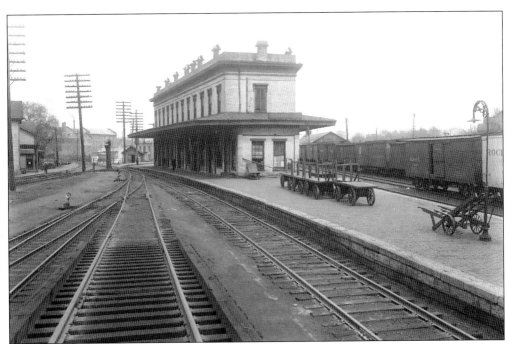

The above view shows the Xenia depot from the west, while the below view shows the telegraph building with the depot behind from the east. In the early 1900s, west of the depot was a roundhouse and coaling station, and farther west at the crossing of the B&O was Greene Tower. Dual water tanks, northwest of the depot, fed water standpipes at the ends of the passenger platform. The passenger depot was demolished in 1955, and a small waiting room was created on the first floor of the telegraph building, which lasted until passenger service was discontinued October 10, 1979. This structure was designated Xenia tower and remained in use until 1986. It came down in 1988. A replica of this building was opened in May 1998 and now serves cyclists on the Greater Miami Trail. (Above, David P. Oroszi collection; below, Gary D. Rolih collection.)

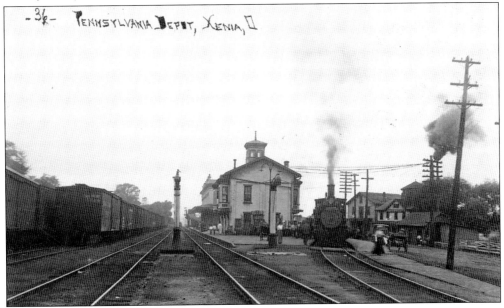

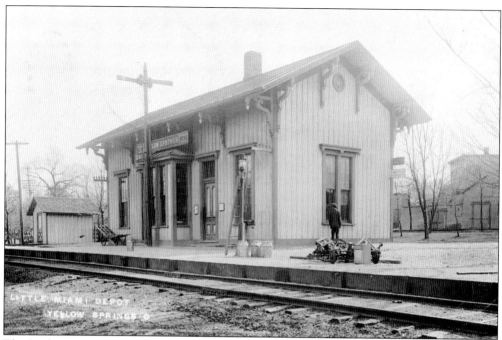

The Little Miami Railroad reached the health resort of Yellow Springs by 1846. By 1870, this combination depot had been erected. This depot was the busiest on the Little Miami's Springfield branch. By 1967, it was a forlorn structure and slated to be burned as a fire department exercise. Luckily some parts of it were saved; other parts disappeared to local farms. Historically minded individuals saw to the building of a replica in 1999, including what could be retrieved of the saved original parts. It also serves cyclists on the Greater Miami Trail. (Gary D. Rolih collection.)

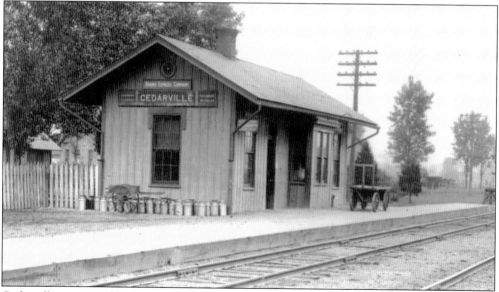

Cedarville was served by this PC&StL plan passenger depot. Beginning in the 1890s, passenger traffic to and from Cedarville College required two waiting rooms, one on either side of the agent's bay-windowed office. A small freight shed was located across the tracks. The depot was gone by the 1970s. (Gary Rauch collection.)

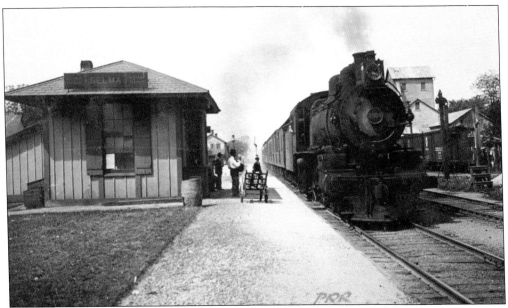

Between Cedarville and the junction with the DT&I at South Charleston was this depot at Selma. Around 1907, a passenger train pulls into the depot. Note the short order board and mail stand to the right. (Author's collection.)

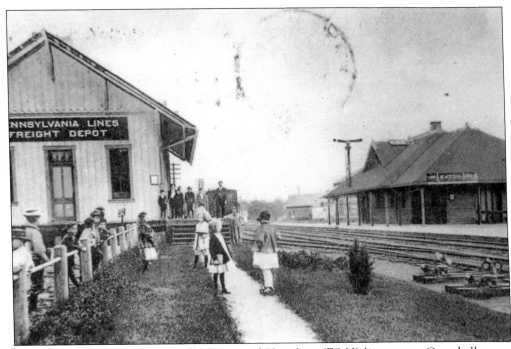

The first depot in Ohio on the old Eaton and Hamilton (E&H) line was at Campbellstown. Besides the depot, the PCC&StL maintained a small telegraph office, called CB Cabin, at East Campbellstown in the early 1900s. The E&H opened through Eaton in May 1853. This frame depot, already in freight use by the early 1900s, was probably the second depot in Eaton. The passenger depot to the right was the third. (Author's collection.)

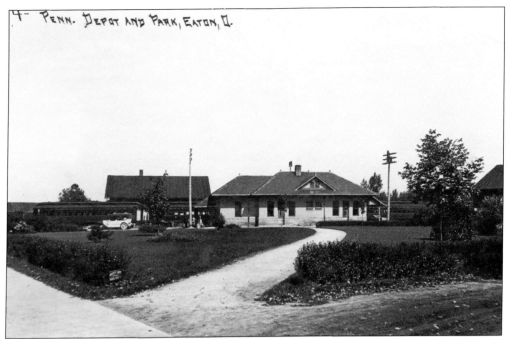

4- Penn. Depot and Park, Eaton, O.

When Eaton's brick depot was built, the old depot became the freight house. At some point the old depot was shortened, when the company removed the old passenger waiting room. A small garden was established on the station grounds. The Eaton passenger depot was an important point on the Richmond line in June 1913 when the evaluation photograph below was taken. By this time, the PCC&StL operated the former Eaton and Hamilton. Both Eaton depots remain as businesses. (Above, author's collection; below, David P. Oroszi collection.)

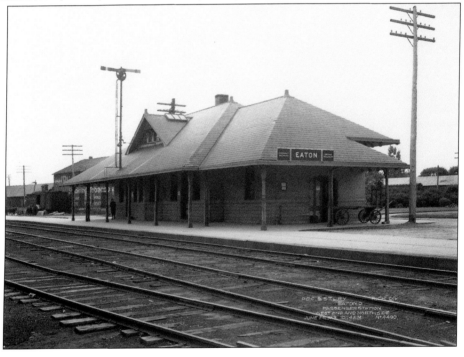

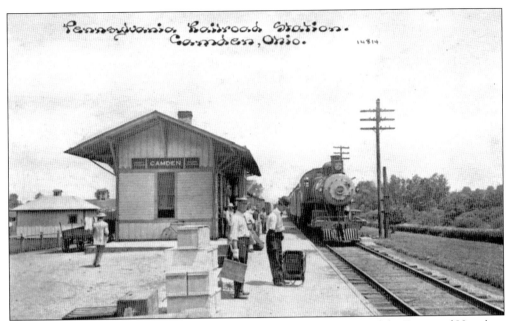

Camden's PRR depot dates to the late 1880s after the PCC&StL purchased the Eaton and Hamilton and constructed a new line from Hamilton into Cincinnati. In this c. 1910 postcard view, a PRR accommodation is about to pick up some travelers. After closing, the depot was moved to a site on Fisher-Twin Road and modified. (Lindsey Scott collection.)

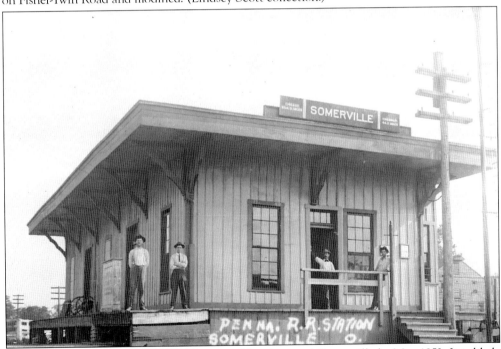

The Eaton and Hamilton operated between Hamilton and Somerville by May 1852. It is likely that this depot dates to the 1850s or 1860s and either is an original E&H design or was built during the tenure of the Cincinnati, Richmond, and Chicago Railroad. The architecture is not typical of PRR structures in this region. (Author's collection.)

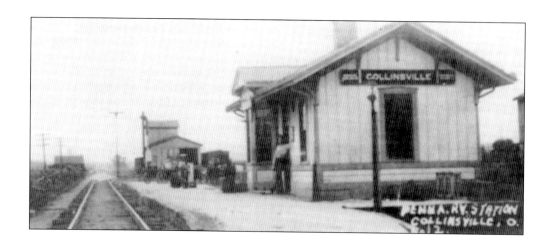

Collinsville's PRR depot is shown in the above c. 1910 postcard view. This is a later depot, probably replacing an original Eaton and Hamilton structure. Seven Mile, below, is of similar architecture to Somerville and probably dates to the time of the Eaton and Hamilton or Cincinnati, Richmond, and Chicago Railroad. (Above, Dan E. Finfrock collection; below, author's collection.)

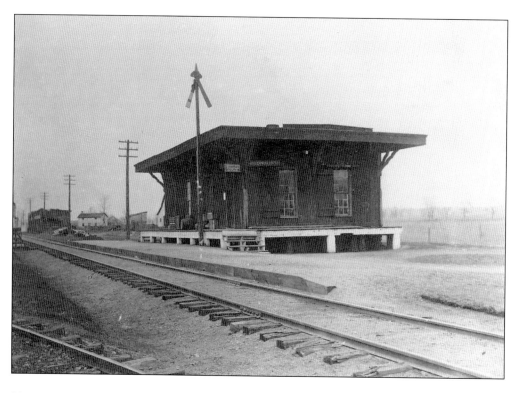

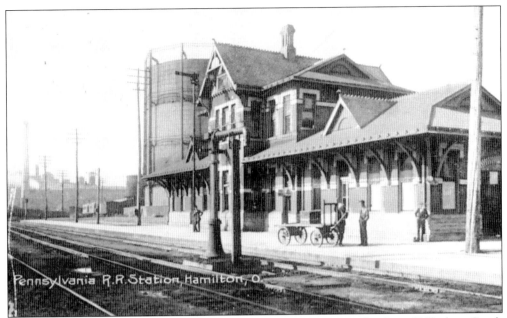

This two-story brick and stone PC&StL passenger depot was opened in June 1888 along South Seventh Street in Hamilton. It replaced an older depot serving the former Eaton and Hamilton. The second floor housed a telegraph office and railroad offices. Ladies' and gentlemen's waiting rooms flanked the agent's office and ticket office. Baggage and express rooms were at opposite ends of the structure. During its heyday, the depot served 15 passenger trains daily. During a PRR modernization program in the mid-1900s, the second story of the Hamilton depot was removed and the depot floor plan rearranged. The last passenger train left in 1971. The depot was unexpectedly demolished January 14–15, 1991, leaving only the nearby 1870 brick freight house as a reminder of the PRR presence in Hamilton. (Above, David P. Oroszi collection; below, 1971 photograph by Charles Garvin.)

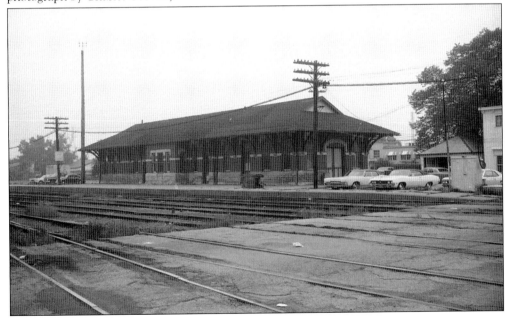

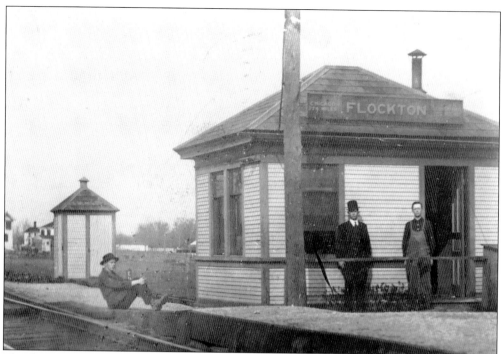

The "boys" pose for the photographer outside the Flockton depot/telegraph office around 1907. Note the town board has mileage to Chicago and Cincinnati. The operator has beautified his place of work by a planting of flowers. The outhouse appears to be a "two-holer." (Author's collection.)

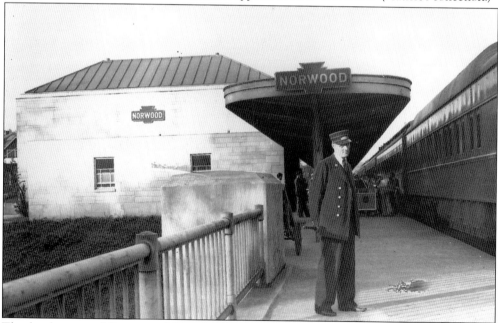

The development of Cincinnati Union Terminal caused the PRR and N&W to seek a new route to the station complex. As part of the project, PRR designed a new suburban depot for Norwood. The art deco limestone structure opened in 1933 and is seen above in the 1940s. (Cincinnati Railroad Club collection.)

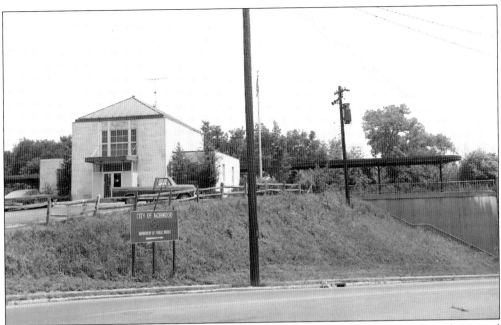

Norwood's new suburban depot served train travelers until 1971, when Amtrak brought an end to passenger service. This view was taken in June 1977. The structure remains in use, adapted as a fraternal lodge. An addition now obscures the west end of the depot. (Photograph by author.)

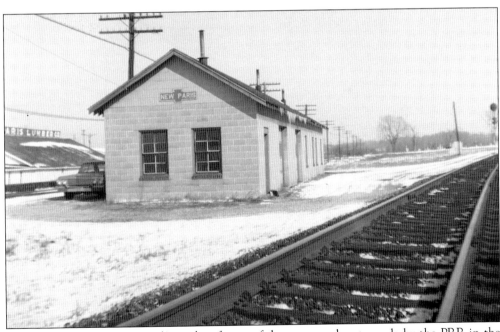

This building shows a typical remake of turn-of-the-century depots made by the PRR in the mid-1900s. The New Paris combination depot was once similar to other depots along the old Dayton and Western Railroad. PRR crews removed ornamental architectural elements, shortened rooflines, cut off bay windows, removed passenger facilities, and sided the buildings with insulated shingles. (1960s photograph by William Wagner.)

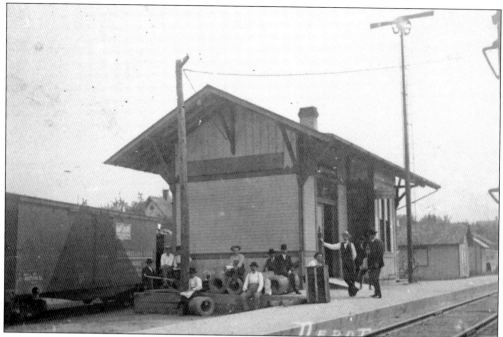

Eldorado was built to standard PCC&StL plans. Compare it to some of the other depots depicted like Brookville, Clare, Kings Mills, and Spring Valley. Rearranging windows and doors, shortening or lengthening passenger and freight rooms, and varying rooflines added variety to the designs. (Gary D. Rolih collection.)

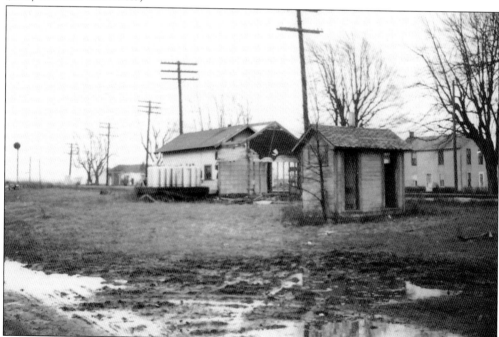

The West Manchester PRR depot is being torn down in this late 1960s view. The PRR also used the Cincinnati Northern depot at the diamond, but this depot disappeared early. A PRR interlocking tower was diagonally across the diamond. (Photograph by Charles Garvin.)

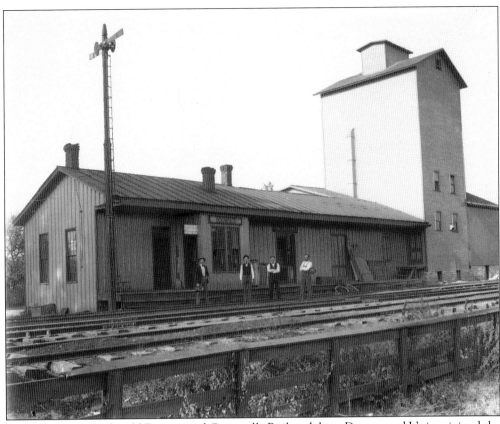

Dodson was where the old Dayton and Greenville Railroad, later Dayton and Union, joined the Dayton and Western line, west of Brookville. A small community developed at the junction served by the above railroad depot. This early 1900s view shows railroad employees posing in front of the vintage depot. The depot is an early design and is adjacent to the grain elevator. The bicycle was probably used to deliver telegrams. Nearby was the telegraph and train order cabin, shown below. (Both, Brookville-Madison Township Historical Society collection.)

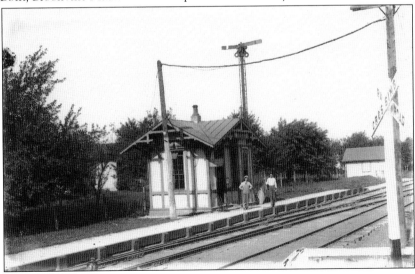

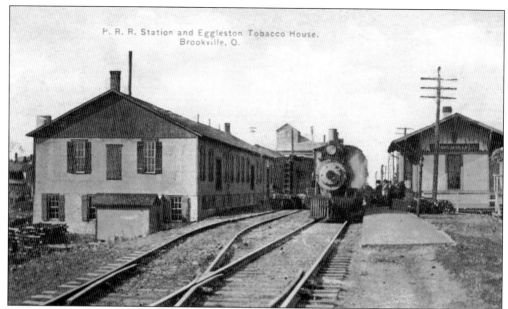

P. R. R. Station and Eggleston Tobacco House.
Brookville, O.

The PRR depots in Brookville (above) and Trotwood (below) have similar histories. When the D&W reached Brookville in 1852, a waiting room and ticket office was opened in the first commercial building. Higgins Station, later Trotwood, was platted in 1898, two years before the above Brookville depot was opened. It was 1912 before the depot below was constructed in Trotwood. Like Brookville, the tickets were originally sold in an early store; a boxcar served as the depot. In 1918, an extension was added to the freight end of the Brookville depot. Trotwood's agency closed in the 1940s; the B&O-PRR agency at Brookville closed in 1974. The Brookville Historical Society opened its museum in their depot on Cusick Avenue in June 1987. After years of commercial use, the Trotwood depot was relocated in 1980 to East Main Street and Broadway Avenue, where it has since been restored. (Above, author's collection; below, 1975 photograph by author.)

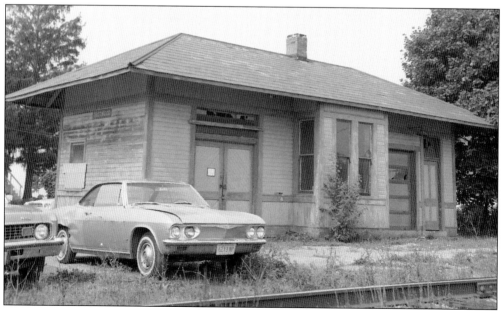

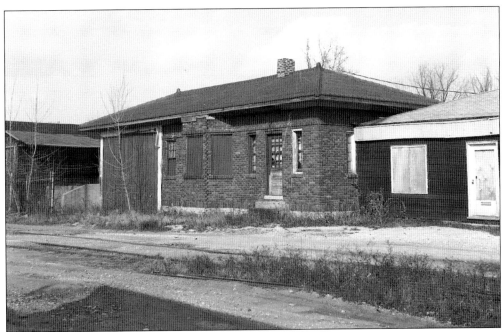

The Dayton, Lebanon, and Cincinnati (DL&C) Railway built this depot around 1912 in Beverton, a few miles south of Lebanon Junction. It was the only brick depot on the line. This view shows the reused depot in November 1975. (Photograph by author.)

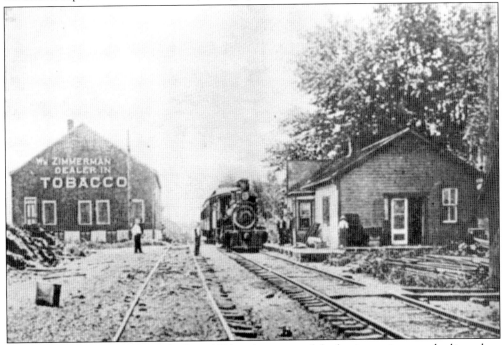

Centerville's DL&C depot was built in 1891 and was one of the busier stations on the line when the dimension stone industry was revitalized by DL&C management. Centerville and south Dayton included the largest concentration of Dayton limestone quarries. This view is from the *Souvenir Booklet*, a promotional book put out by the DL&C in 1912. (Richard A. Lenehan collection.)

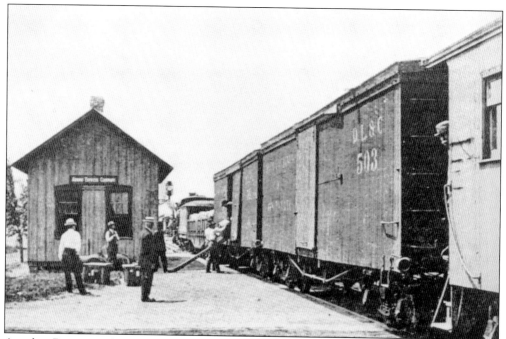

Another Dayton, Lebanon, and Cincinnati depot was constructed in Lytle in 1891. The Lytle depot handled mainly drainage tile, Dayton stone, and lumber. The view is from the *Souvenir Booklet* promotional book put out by the DL&C in 1912. (Richard A. Lenehan collection.)

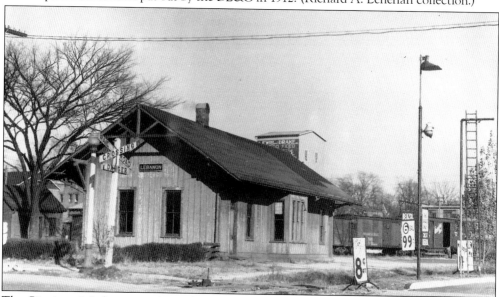

The Cincinnati, Lebanon, and Northern opened this passenger depot at South Broadway and South Streets in Lebanon in 1881. Separate gentlemen's and ladies' waiting rooms were on opposite sides of a bay-windowed central station agent's office. After the PRR took over the CL&N in 1896, the depot was moved farther back from South Broadway, so that trains would less frequently block the street crossing. Passenger service to Lebanon ended January 31, 1934. The depot was demolished in 1960 and replaced with a smaller building moved in from Kings Mills for the freight agent. (Richard A. Lenehan collection.)

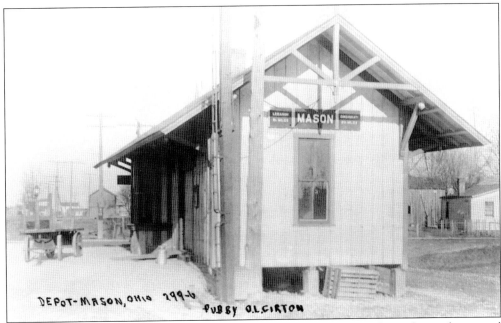

CL&N's 1881 Mason depot was built to a similar plan as Lebanon, but a few architectural tweaks distinguished it. Passenger service, except for one mixed train daily between Lebanon and Cincinnati, was discontinued in the spring of 1931. The Mason depot was a busy place, especially in the morning and early evening when Cincinnati commuters filled the platform. (Gary D. Rolih collection.)

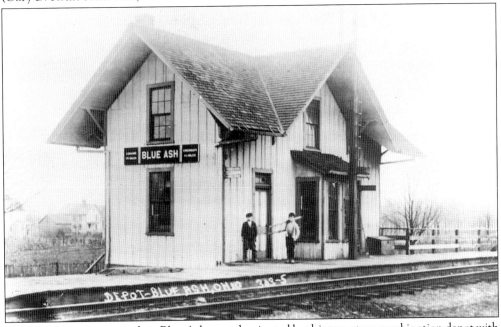

The CL&N station grounds at Blue Ash were dominated by this two-story combination depot with a second-floor apartment for the station agent. A twin to this depot once served Kennedy (next page). Blue Ash marked the wye with the short Montgomery branch, which served Montgomery commuters until 1926. (Author's collection.)

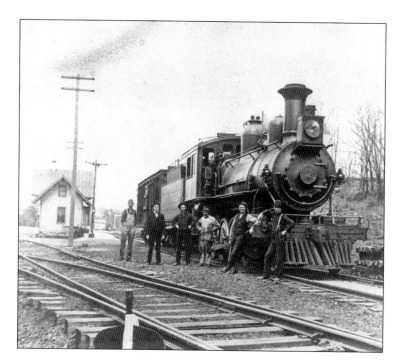

The Cincinnati, Lebanon, and Northern Railway built a two-story frame depot at Kennedy to a similar floor plan as the Blue Ash structure. The second floor provided living space for the agent. (Dan E. Finfrock collection.)

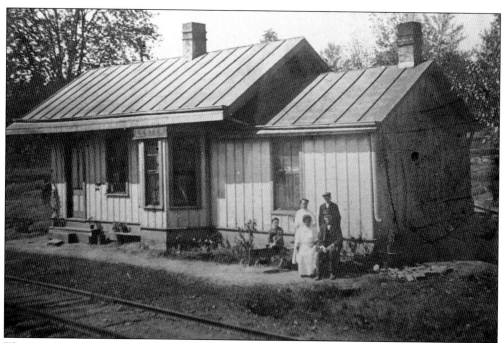

The Cincinnati, Lebanon, and Northern's (CL&N) depot at Lester Road, north of Norwood, was atypical among the line's depots. The addition on the right was the caretaker's residence. The Morton Ketcham family, posed in front, was the station maintainers between 1906 and 1910. (Richard A. Lenehan collection.)

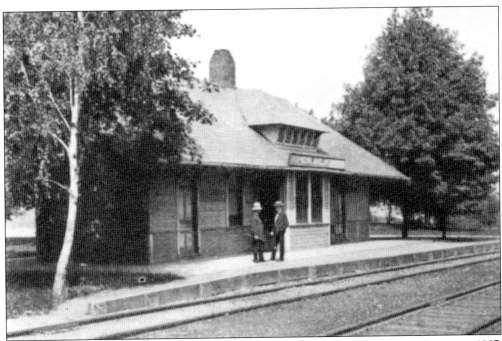

Norwood commuters began a campaign to construct a depot at a site on Hopkins Avenue in 1887. The next year construction began. The CL&N furnished some of the materials and carpenters, but the Hopkins Avenue Depot Company provided the funds. Construction took place at a rapid pace—the official opening was August 1, 1888. The depot served the community until the end of passenger service in 1934. The Hopkins Avenue structure remains in business use along the abandoned right-of-way. (Author's collection.)

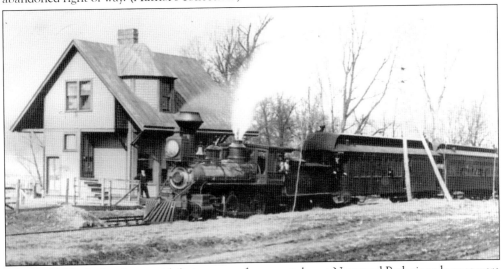

The CL&N built this depot with living space for a caretaker at Norwood Park since homes were not yet readily available in this rural area south of Norwood. The caretaker kept the waiting room clean and the stove stoked in the winter; no tickets were sold. A narrow-gauge passenger train sits at the Norwood Park depot in 1887. The dirt road in the foreground is now Lafayette Avenue. The farmland in the background would soon become part of several new subdivisions. (Richard A. Lenehan collection.)

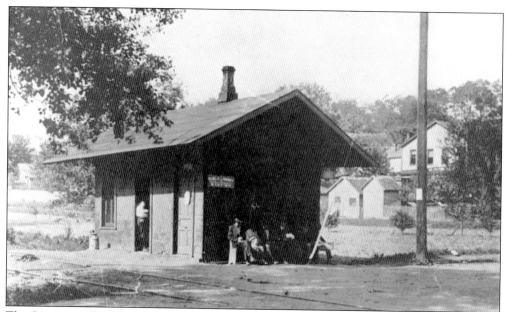

The Cincinnati, Georgetown, and Portsmouth Railroad depot at California (above photograph) also contained the town's post office and library. During the 1913 flood, water rose to its eaves, however, the damage was repaired and it returned to use. The original depot at Mount Washington was built to company plans for a small town combination depot. It was a utilitarian design with a standard pitched roof and lacking the overhang and bay window of most railroad depots. The view below shows the depot after it was moved to California Junction in 1902 and converted to house the station agent. It was from here that trains left the main for the Cincinnati Waterworks, California, and the amusement park at Coney Island. Evidence of the CG&P is pretty much obliterated in this area today. (Both, Stephen B. Smalley collection.)

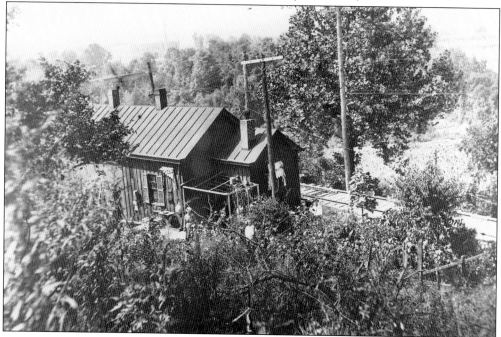

Five

OTHER LINES

September 1876 marked the beginning of construction of the narrow-gauge Cincinnati and Portsmouth Railroad from Cincinnati into the hills of Clermont County. Financial problems came long before the railroad even reached Bethel. The new owners renamed it the Cincinnati, Georgetown, and Portsmouth Railroad in 1880. In 1902, the route was changed to standard gauge and converted to electric power. The interurbans made their last runs in 1935—a victim of the Great Depression.

The narrow-gauge Springfield, Jackson, and Pomeroy Railroad opened for passenger service between Springfield and Washington Court House in January 1878. The line was standard gauged in 1879 and after several reorganizations became the Detroit, Toledo, and Ironton Railway. During the 1890s, an extension to Cincinnati was planned to run from Jeffersonville on the mainline to a point on the Little Miami Railroad. The line was completed to Kingman by 1894, but the connection was never made. In 1892, the DT&I built north from Springfield.

The Kingman Branch used a portion of the roadbed of the narrow-gauge Waynesville, Port William, and Jeffersonville Railroad (built in 1877) from Jeffersonville to a junction with the narrow-gauge Dayton and Southeastern. After two reorganizations, the Cincinnati, Columbus, and Hocking Valley took over in 1881 and immediately upgraded the line to standard gauge. Financial problems continued, and the tracks were removed in 1887.

The 6-foot-gauge Atlantic and Great Western Railroad also reached into Southwest Ohio, building a line from Marion to Springfield to Dayton and acquiring trackage rights into Cincinnati from the CH&D. The line was converted to standard gauge in 1880 as part of its reorganization as the New York, Pennsylvania, and Ohio Railroad. This route became the Erie Railroad in 1895. Much of the so-called Dayton Branch has been torn up.

One of the later lines to be built in Southwest Ohio was the Chicago, Cincinnati, and Louisville, which opened in 1904. It became the shortest rail route between Cincinnati and Chicago. The line became the C&O of Indiana in 1910 and just the C&O in 1933. The Ohio portion of the line has been abandoned.

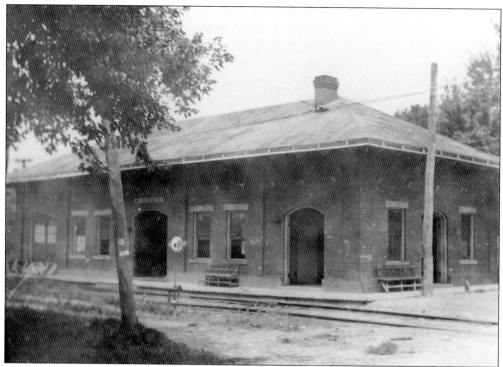

This substantial building replaced the frame depot at Mount Washington when the line underwent electrification and conversion to standard gauge in 1902. It is constructed to typical plans of a combined depot and electrical substation. The structure survives as home to the American Legion on Sutton Avenue. (Stephen B. Smalley collection.)

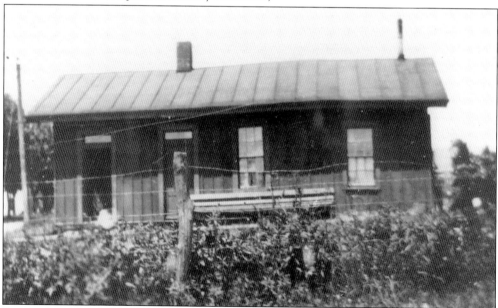

Fruit Hill was appropriately named for a farming community. The depot dates to the 1880s and was built to a standard plan of the Cincinnati, Georgetown, and Portsmouth. The depot was discontinued as an agency in 1926. (Stephen B. Smalley collection.)

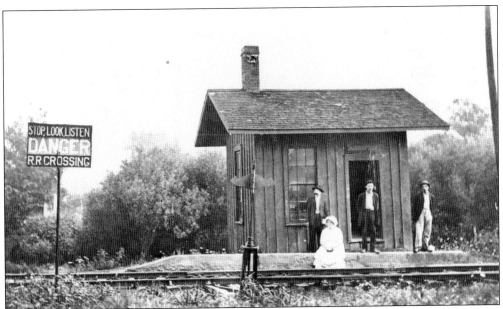

Summerside had one of the smaller depots, other than three-sided shelters, on the Cincinnati, Georgetown, and Portsmouth. Located here during the narrow-gauge days was a large wind-driven pump station and water tank, unfortunately out of this view. (Stephen B. Smalley collection.)

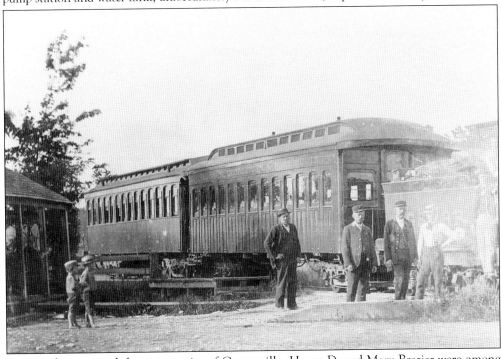

Braziers depot served the community of Centerville. Henry D. and Mary Brazier were among those to provide land for a station. This Cincinnati, Georgetown, and Portsmouth depot was the next stop south of Lake Allyn. The building to the left served as the post office and railroad depot. This 1880s view shows the Hamlet accommodation, a daily passenger run from Hamlet into Cincinnati. (Stephen B. Smalley collection.)

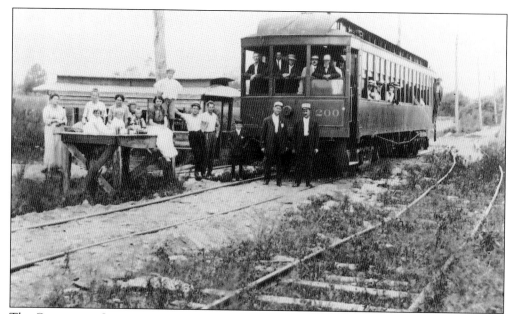

The Cincinnati, Georgetown, and Portsmouth positioned an old narrow-gauge coach to serve as the depot at Wiltsee. Perhaps the people are on a church outing. The wooden platform is for milk cans from local farms. (Stephen B. Smalley collection.)

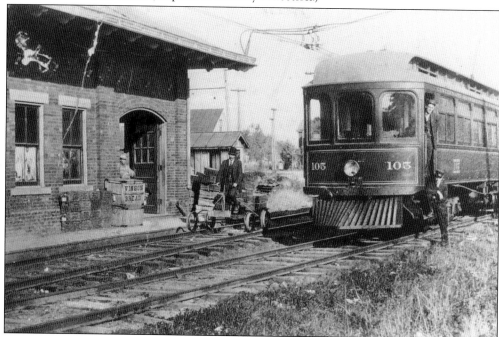

The Cincinnati, Georgetown, and Portsmouth entered Bethel in July 1881. This is the second depot constructed at Bethel, the earlier one was a standard plan frame combination depot. This substantial building on South Street was constructed as the line was electrified and housed apparatus for boosting the current in the overhead trolley wires. Motorman Connie Baldwin (in car) and conductor Leonard Hauck pose for the photographer around 1903. After closing, it later became a church. (Author's collection.)

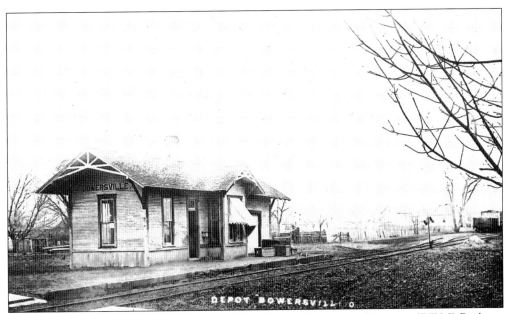

Bowersville was on the Kingman branch of the Detroit, Toledo, and Ironton (DT&I) Railway. The depot is similar in architecture to a number of mainline DT&I depots. Reportedly the depot was relocated after its closing. (Author's collection.)

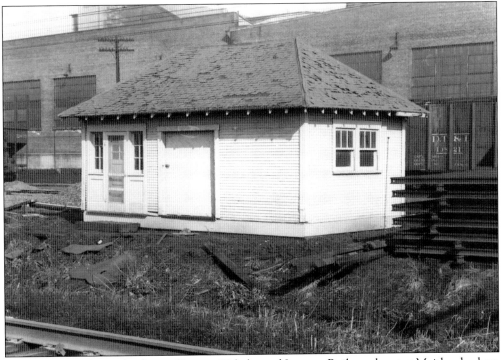

This 1954 view shows the former Detroit, Toledo, and Ironton Railway depot at Maitland, where the DT&I and Erie Railroad cross on the northwest side of Springfield. By the 1950s, it served as an office for DT&I's police. (Eldon Neff photograph.)

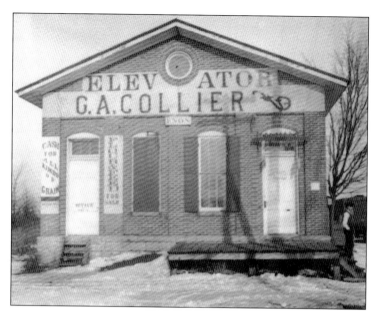

For some unknown reason the Erie chose to use an existing store building at Enon rather than constructing a separate depot. This photograph was recorded in 1922 by an Erie Railroad photographer as part of the nationwide railroad property evaluation program. The Big Four apparently also used this as a depot. The building remains to the north of the interstate. (Erie Railroad photograph, author's collection.)

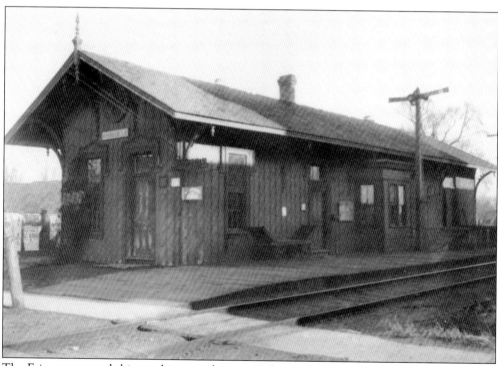

The Erie constructed this combination depot in Osborn in the late 1800s. By the early 1900s, Erie passengers were using a relocated and modified Big Four depot. The Erie building became used for storage and freight. The construction of Huffman Dam put Osborn in the floodwater holding area. The Erie and New York Central tracks were relocated, as was much of downtown Osborn in 1921. The Erie depot was apparently torn down instead of being moved. (1910 Erie Railroad photograph, author's collection.)

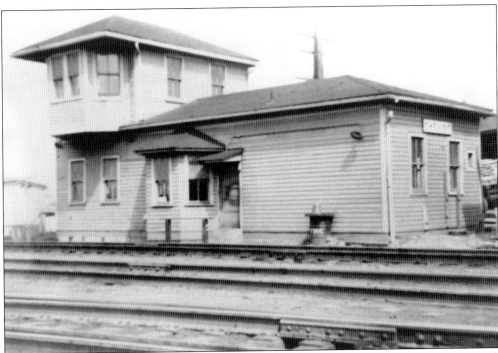

Once called Summit, Cheviot on the west side of Cincinnati, was the site of a major C&O yard. This view shows the depot-yard office. This was later replaced by a modern brickyard office. Although this was a unique structure, the depots on the Ohio portion of the Chicago, Cincinnati, and Louisville (CC&L) were all built to the same plan. (C&O Historical Society collection.)

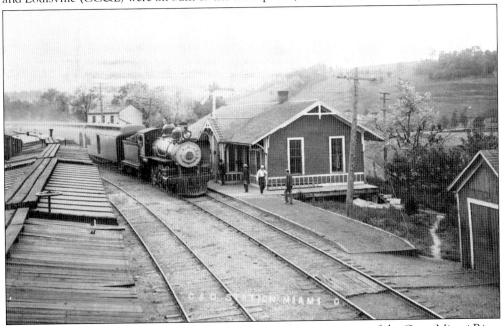

The CC&L standard plan is exhibited by the depot at Miami just east of the Great Miami River and the town of Miamitown on the west side of the valley. The depot was erected in 1904 with the opening of the line. (Author's collection.)

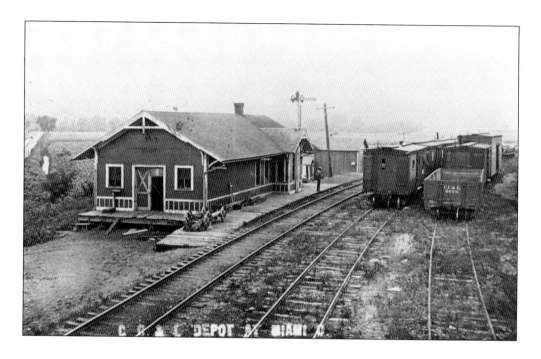

The opposite end of the standard plan depot at Miami is shown in this *c.* 1907 view. The depot at Fernald (below), also opened in 1904, was the last of these depots to be torn down because of the business generated by the uranium plant. Tracks from Cincinnati to Fernald were taken up in 1978. (Above, David P. Oroszi collection; below, author's collection.)

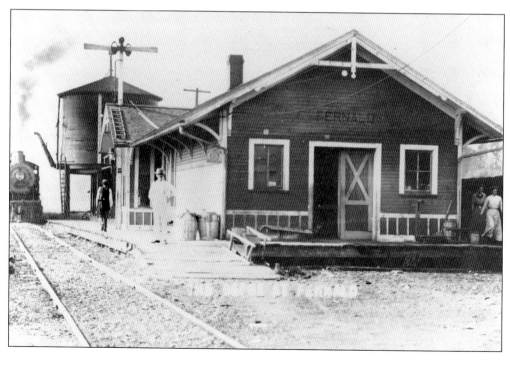

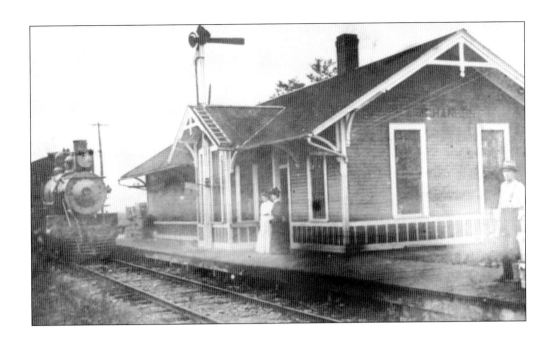

Farther north was the village of Shandon. Excursions to Cincinnati to visit the zoo, take in a ball game, or enjoy any number of other city attractions were offered most Sundays and holidays. The ticket from Shandon cost 45¢. In 1946, Shandon (above) and Okeana (below) were the only C&O depots still offering passenger service between Cincinnati and the Indiana line. (Both, author's collection.)

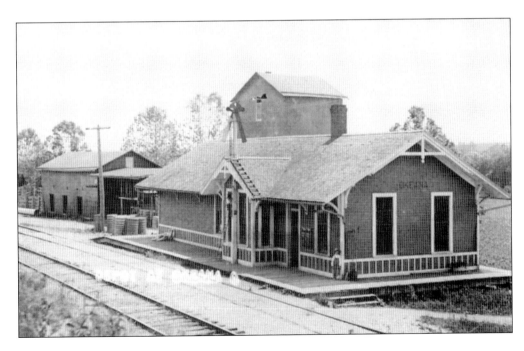

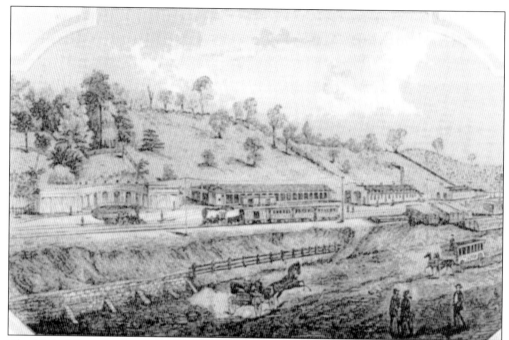

The Little Miami Railroad opened its first Cincinnati passenger depot, above, in 1843. The depot was located far east of the downtown in Pendleton, the location of the line's shops. The passenger cars were hauled to the downtown by mules; steam locomotives were not allowed in the downtown district. As was a common design of the earliest depots, this barn-like depot covered two tracks. In 1848, this building was converted to other railroad use, and a new depot, below, was constructed at east Front and Kilgore Streets. The second depot was larger but of similar architecture. (Above, author's collection; below, Cincinnati Railroad Club collection.)

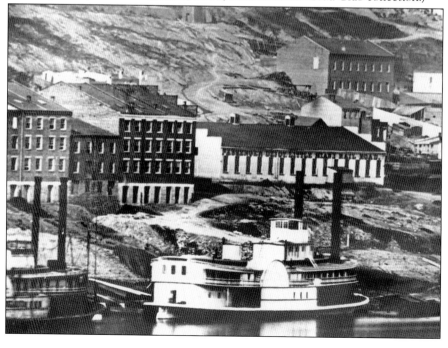

Six

CINCINNATI

The Queen City was first served by the Little Miami Railroad, which opened a line to Xenia in 1844. The second line, the Cincinnati and Hamilton Railroad, later the Cincinnati, Hamilton, and Dayton, opened between Cincinnati and Dayton in 1851. The Ohio and Mississippi Railroad linked Cincinnati to East St. Louis in 1857. The Marietta and Cincinnati Railroad first entered the city in 1854. The Cincinnati and Indiana Railroad opened down the Whitewater Valley to Cincinnati in 1863. The Atlantic and Great Western Railroad entered Cincinnati by trackage rights on the CH&D in the early 1860s. In 1872, the Cleveland, Columbus, Cincinnati, and Indianapolis (CCC&I) Railroad opened between Cincinnati and Springfield. The Cincinnati, Georgetown, and Portsmouth Railroad began construction as the Cincinnati and Portsmouth in 1876. From 1901 to its abandonment in 1935, it functioned as an interurban line serving small communities to the east of the city. The Cincinnati Northern Railway formed in 1880 to complete a narrow-gauge line into Cincinnati. This line became the Cincinnati, Lebanon, and Northern Railway in 1885. The Louisville and Nashville also served Cincinnati by 1872, but their main passenger facility was across the Ohio River in Newport, Kentucky. The wide-gauge Cincinnati Southern Railway (later Southern) formed a connection between Cincinnati and Chattanooga in 1880. The narrow-gauge Cincinnati and Eastern Railroad linked Cincinnati with Portsmouth in 1884. This route became part of the Norfolk and Western Railway in 1901. The year 1888 marked the opening of two future Pennsylvania Railroad lines—the Cincinnati, Richmond, and Chicago between Hamilton and Rendcomb Junction and the Cincinnati and Richmond between Red Bank and Hamilton. The Chesapeake and Ohio Railway entered the city from Kentucky in 1889.

Among the lines originally having passenger depots in Cincinnati were the C&O, Little Miami, PC&StL, Ohio and Mississippi, CH&D, Big Four, CL&N, and CG&P. Although most served more than one railroad, their wide scattering across the city made passenger transfers difficult. The grand solution was the opening of Cincinnati Union Terminal in 1933.

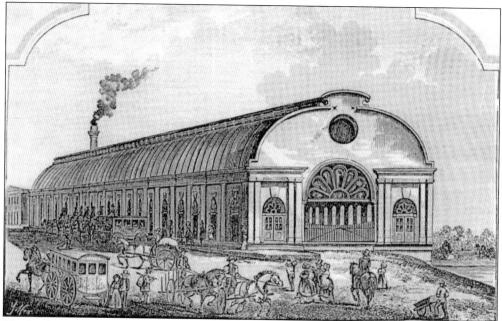

The Little Miami Railroad opened a third barn-like depot (above) on the riverfront near Butler Street in 1853. In the early 1880s, the Little Miami converted the Butler Street depot to a freight house and began using the new 1881 PC&StL depot (below) at East Pearl and Butler Streets. The depot consisted of a two-story towered head house of brick and stone with a train shed covering six tracks. Trains of the Cincinnati and Muskingum Valley and the Cincinnati, Richmond, and Chicago also used this depot. By 1916, the station was serving around 50 daily trains. (Above, Public Library of Cincinnati and Hamilton County collection; below, Gary D. Rolih collection.)

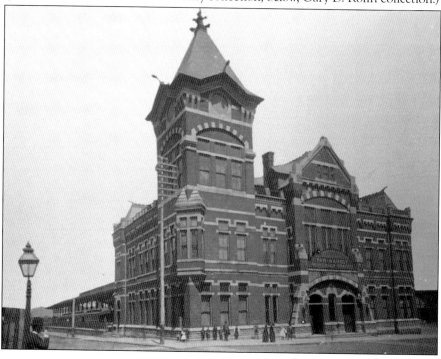

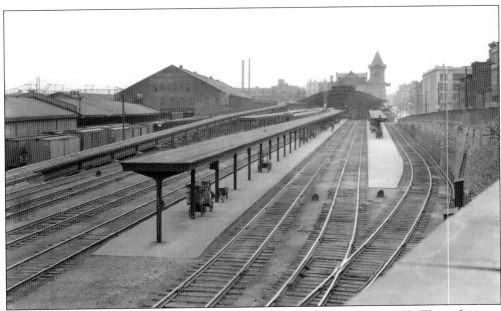

The above view of the train shed at Pearl Street Station was taken in 1933. Through trains of the N&W also used this depot. The Pennsylvania Railroad built a suburban depot (shown below around 1930) in 1905–1907 between Pearl Street Station and Pendleton off Columbia and Eastern Avenues at Torrence Road. The tower encloses an elevator shaft. The depot served many of Cincinnati's socialites and politicians who mostly lived in nearby East Walnut Hills. The last PRR passenger train left these two depots April 1, 1933, with the opening of Cincinnati Union Terminal. Within a couple years these depots were gone as well. (Above, Dan E. Finfrock collection; below, Cincinnati Railroad Club collection.)

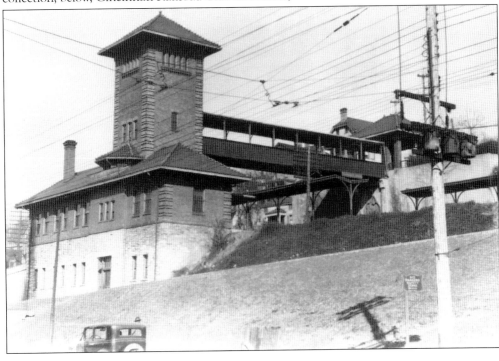

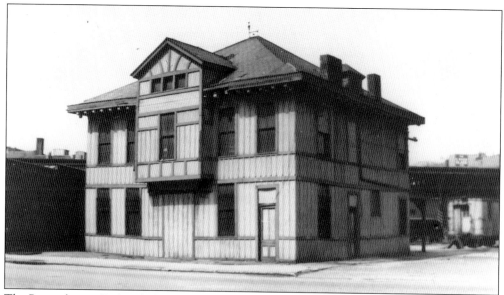

The Pennsylvania Railroad also maintained a small depot at Carrell Street near the Cincinnati terminal of the CG&P. The Cincinnati, Lebanon, and Northern opened a new depot at Court Street (above and below) in December 1885. This replaced an earlier Cincinnati Northern Railway depot on the southeast corner of Court and Broadway Streets. The N&W also used this depot for some of its local trains. Passenger service ended here in 1933 with the opening of Cincinnati Union Terminal. The depot, shown above in the 1940s, remained in storage use until its demolition in 1952. (Above, Richard A. Lenehan collection; below, 1920s view, N&W Historical Photograph Collection, Virginia Tech University Library.)

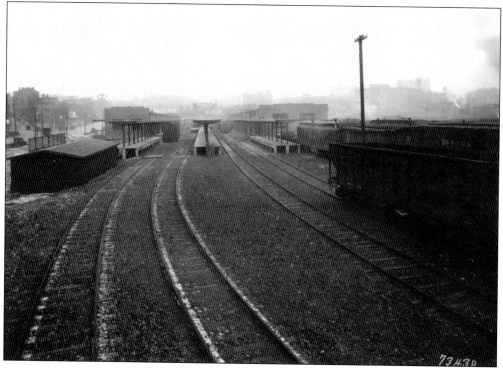

The CH&D opened the passenger depot, at right, at the corner of West Fifth and Baymiller (Hoadley) Streets in 1864–1865, replacing an earlier depot built in 1851. The 1868 view below shows the rear of the above 1865 depot. The left-hand building is the train shed of the 1865 depot, the middle one is the 1851 passenger depot converted to a through freight house, and the right-hand structure is another through freight house. Note the dual-gauge rails to accommodate the wide gauge of Atlantic and Great Western trains that, along with the standard-gauge Marietta and Cincinnati, also used the CH&D facilities. (Right, Gary D. Rolih collection; below, the Hays T. Watkins Research Library, B&O Museum, Inc.)

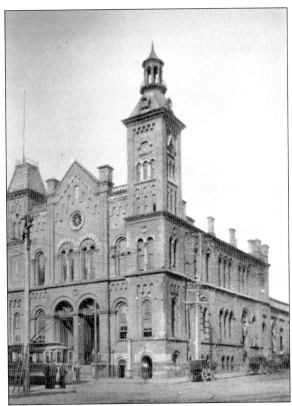

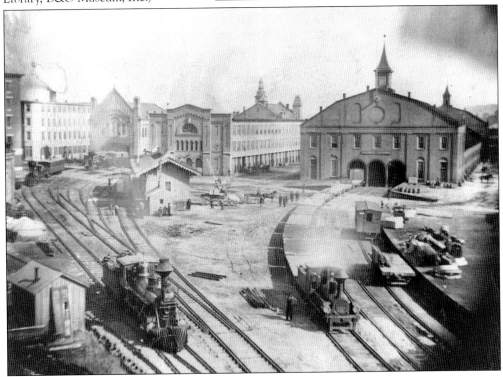

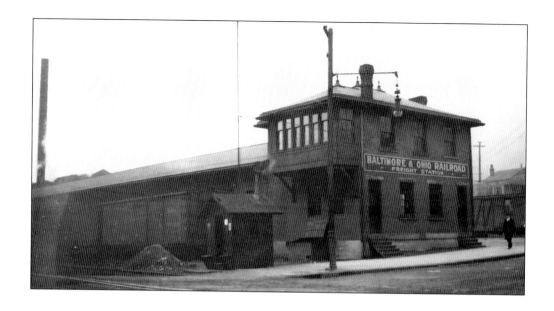

The CH&D also maintained depots at Gest Street (above) and Eighth Street (below). The Gest Street structure, shown in 1918, originally served passengers but in later years was used for only freight. It was removed in 1976. The Eighth Street depot was a commuter depot located below the Eighth Street viaduct that disappeared in the 1930s. (Above, the Hays T. Watkins Research Library, B&O Museum, Inc.; below, author's collection.)

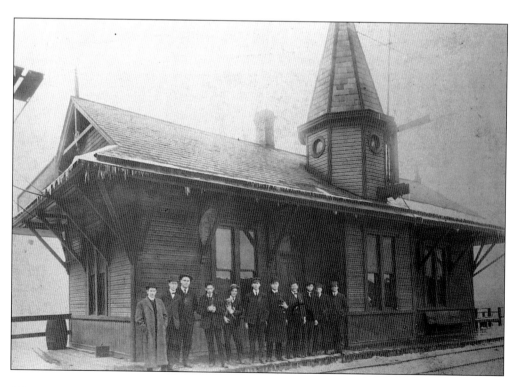

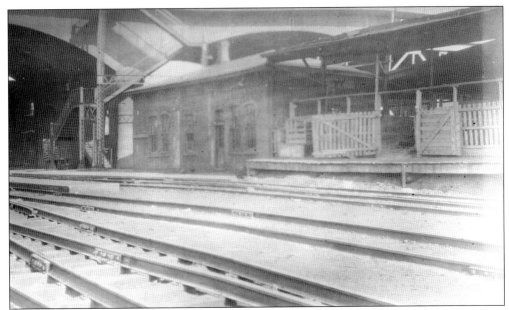

The CH&D's Stockyards depot, above, was located on Cincinnati's north side. By 1918, the depot was hidden under a viaduct and surrounded by smelly stockyards. Cincinnati Junction (below) once sported this towered depot. The CH&D, B&OSW, and Southern lines junctured at this point. The below view dates to 1898, when CH&D workers were in the process of clearing flood debris from the station grounds. (Above, the Hays T. Watkins Research Library, B&O Museum, Inc.; below, Dan E. Finfrock collection.)

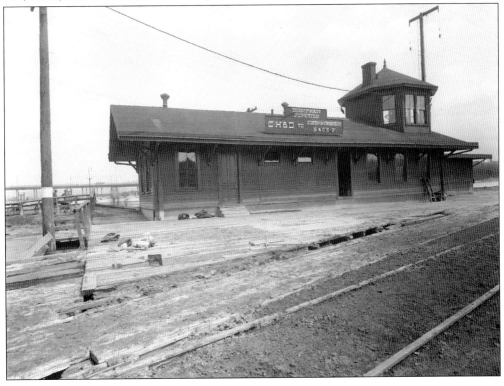

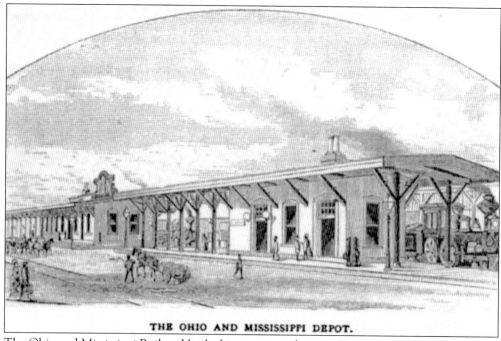

THE OHIO AND MISSISSIPPI DEPOT.

The Ohio and Mississippi Railroad built this passenger depot at West Front and Mill Streets in 1873 on the far west side of Cincinnati. The depot had gentlemen's and ladies' waiting rooms, a restaurant, and telegraph office. The second building down the track was a freight-baggage facility. In the 1870s, the O&M was running six daily passenger trains each direction. Plum Street depot of the Indianapolis, Cincinnati, and Louisville Railroad was built in 1863 at the corner of Pearl Street and Central Avenue. In the 1870s, twenty-three daily passenger trains used the depot, including those of the CCC&I. With the opening of nearby Central Union Station, the depot became a Big Four warehouse until its demise in 1961. (Both, illustrations from D. J. Kenny's 1875 *Illustrated Cincinnati*.)

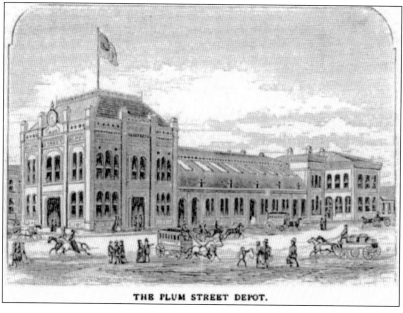

THE PLUM STREET DEPOT.

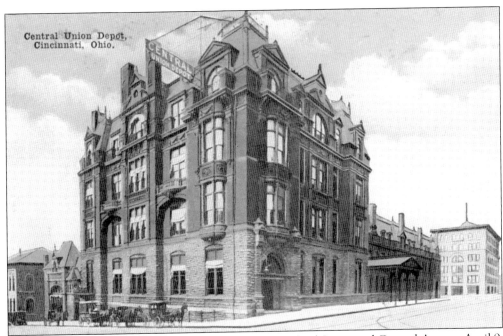

Central Union Depot,
Cincinnati, Ohio.

Central Union Depot, above, opened at the corner of Third Street and Central Avenue April 9, 1883. The Cincinnati, Indianapolis, St. Louis, and Chicago Railroad was behind the construction of this depot. Joining this line within the first year of operation were the CCC&I; O&M; and the Cincinnati, Washington, and Baltimore (formerly the Marietta and Cincinnati). In later years, Central Union Depot served trains of the Big Four, B&O, and Southern. The train shed sheltered eight tracks. The depot lasted until the opening of Union Terminal. The Big Four also had a depot at Mill Creek (below). The bridge in the foreground is for the connector line to the B&OSW (former O&M). (Above, author's collection; below, Dan E. Finfrock collection.)

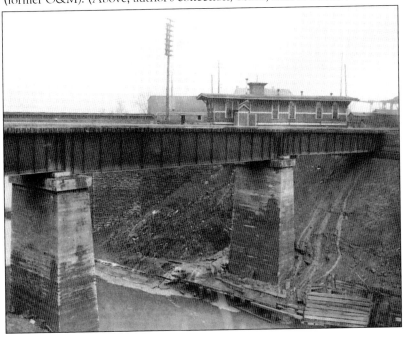

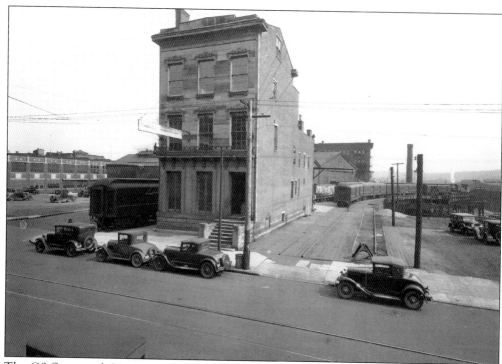

The C&O entered Cincinnati from Covington, Kentucky, in 1889 on a massive bridge and purchased a former 1869 row house in 1891 to serve as their passenger depot on Fourth Street near Smith Street. The plan had been to run into Central Union Station, but by this time it was already accommodating more trains than it could handle. The converted depot closed with the opening of Cincinnati Union Terminal in 1933. Above is a front view and below a rear view showing the two passenger tracks that ran into the station. Note the elevated tracks of the C&O in the background. (Both, Dan E. Finfrock collection.)

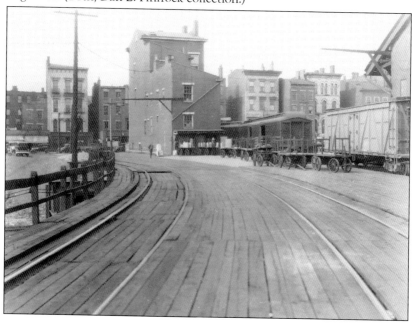

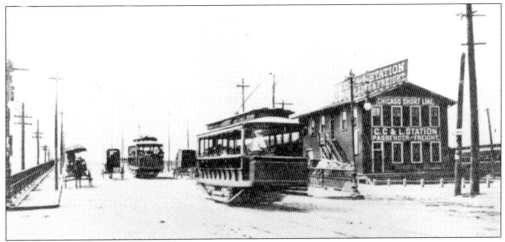

The Chicago, Cincinnati, and Louisville opened its depot at West Eighth Street and McLean Avenue on the west side of the city in 1904. The company heavily advertised the fact that it was indeed Cincinnati's shortest rail route to Chicago. (Dan E. Finfrock collection.)

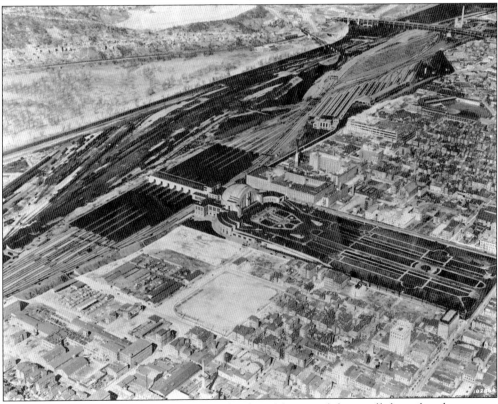

By the early 1900s, a number of plans were developed for consolidating all the railroad passenger facilities in downtown Cincinnati into one grand complex. By 1928, Cincinnati saw some 20,000 passengers come and go from the city's widely scattered depots. The Cincinnati Union Terminal Company was formed, and a site was chosen in the valley of Mill Creek. In 1933, this extensive complex opened to great fanfare. (N&W Historical Photograph Collection, Virginia Tech University Library.)

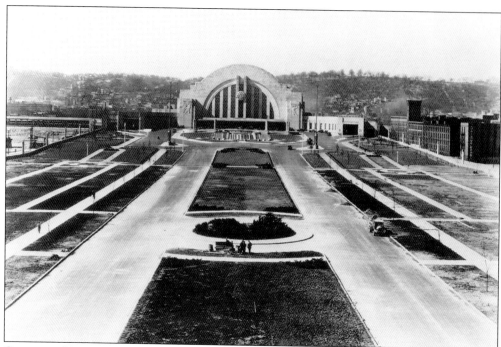

Cincinnati Union Terminal was widely acclaimed for its design and efficiency. The above April 1933 view looks west on Lincoln Parkway to the entrance to the great rotunda. Directly in front of the depot is the yet uncompleted fountain. Below is a 1972 view of the platform shelters just before Amtrak's *George Washington* abandoned the terminal in favor of a new depot on River Road. The platform canopies and train concourse was demolished in 1973. (Above, N&W Historical Photograph Collection, Virginia Tech University Library; below, photograph by Charles Garvin.)

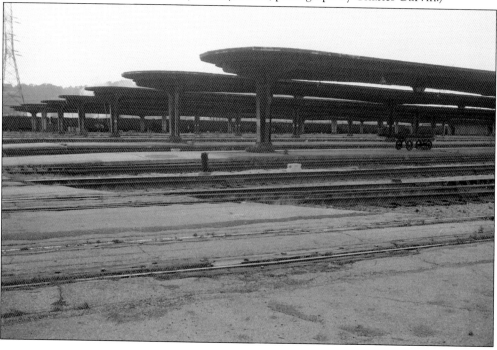

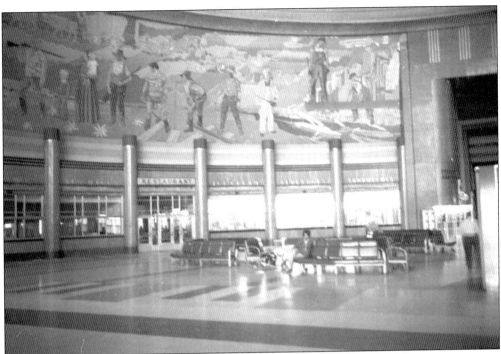

The interior of Cincinnati Union Terminal was as spectacular as the exterior. The main concourse or rotunda, above, was a spacious area surrounded by colorful murals. This 1972 view shows the restaurant area. On the north side were 18 ticket windows. Below is the centrally located magazine stand and information booth. After railroad use ended, steps were taken to preserve the remaining parts of the terminal. Some of the murals were relocated to the Greater Cincinnati Airport. The terminal was opened as a shopping mall in the early 1980s. In 1990, it opened as Museum Center. (Both, photographs by Charles Garvin.)

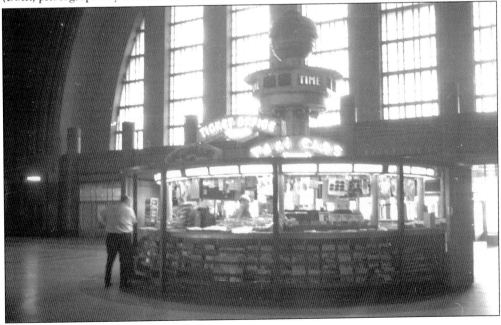

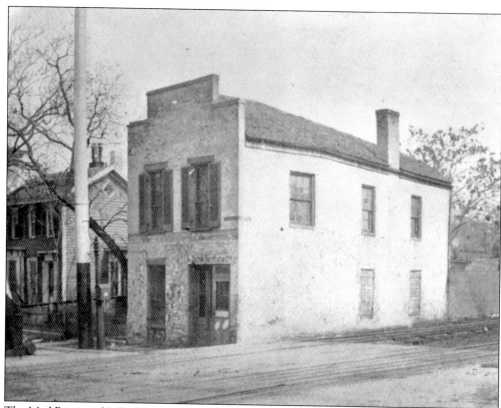

The Mad River and Lake Erie converted the above building to serve as a waiting room and ticket office at the northeast corner of Sixth and Jefferson Streets in Dayton in 1851. This depot was still in use in 1895 when the *Dayton Daily Journal* referred to it as the old "coffin" because of obscured views of approaching trains. In the mid-1850s, the Cincinnati, Hamilton, and Dayton erected the covered passenger depot below. When first built, there were large doors on each end. By the time of this 1899 photograph looking west, the depot was too small to handle the traffic. (Above, Lutzenberger Photograph collection, Dayton Metro Library; below, Dan E. Finfrock collection.)

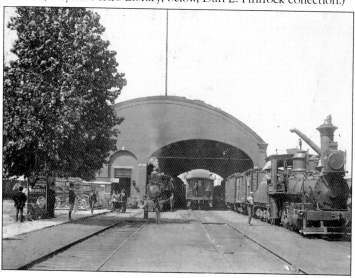

Eight

DAYTON AND SPRINGFIELD

The wide-gauge Cincinnati, Hamilton, and Dayton and Mad River and Lake Erie Railroads reached Dayton in 1851. The next year, the Dayton and Michigan Railroad began to build north up the Great Miami River Valley. In 1853, Dayton was connected to Indiana and points west by the Dayton and Western Railroad. The Dayton, Xenia, and Belpre Railroad opened a line to Xenia in 1858. By 1864, the Atlantic and Great Western Railroad reached Dayton from Springfield, becoming the Erie Railroad in 1895. The Cleveland, Columbus, Cincinnati, and Indianapolis Railroad provided another connection to Cincinnati in 1872. In 1877, the narrow-gauge Dayton and Southeastern Railroad opened to the coalfields of southeast Ohio. Another narrow-gauge line, the Dayton, Covington, and Piqua Railroad, built up the Stillwater River Valley in 1878. Most of the early lines had a separate depot, but by the mid-1850s, the CH&D oversaw the erection of the first union station. These depots were replaced by Dayton Union Station, which was officially dedicated in 1900. Today the only passenger depot in town is the Bowling Green depot relocated from northwest Ohio to Carillon Park.

Springfield was first connected by rail when the Little Miami Railroad built in from the south in 1846. The Mad River and Lake Erie Railroad connected the city to Sandusky in 1848. By 1853, the city was connected to London by the Springfield and London Railroad and, in 1862, to Delaware by the Springfield, Mt. Vernon, and Pittsburgh Railway. The year 1872 brought the Cincinnati and Springfield Railroad and a connection to Cincinnati. The next railroad to reach Springfield was the broad-gauge Atlantic and Great Western Railroad in 1864, later the Dayton Branch of the Erie Railroad. The narrow-gauge Springfield, Jackson, and Pomeroy Railroad began a route to the coalfields in 1877 and eventually became part of the Detroit, Toledo, and Ironton Railroad in 1914. The Big Four, DT&I, Erie, and Pennsylvania Railroads all maintained passenger depots in Springfield. All have since been demolished.

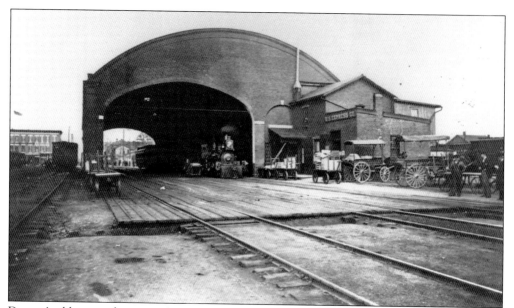

Dayton's old union depot was located at Ludlow and Sixth Streets. It housed a baggage room, ticket office, ladies' and gentlemen's waiting rooms, telegraph office, and a restaurant on the south side of the enclosed platform. The above view looks east and shows an added express office. Like the early covered depots in Cincinnati, little attempt was made to prevent smoke and soot within the train shed. Below is a west view in 1899. This depot would soon be replaced by Dayton Union Station, seen under construction to the north of the tracks. (Both, David P. Oroszi collection.)

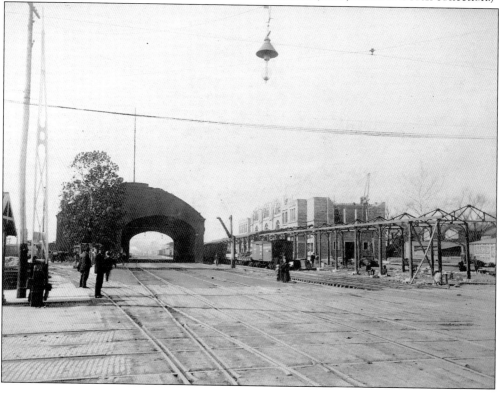

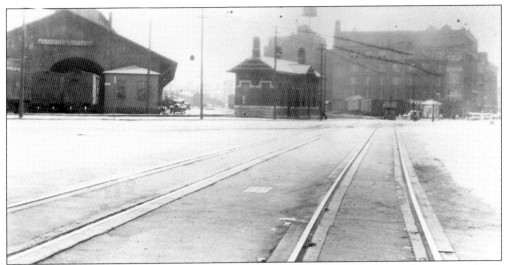

The Pittsburg, Cincinnati, Chicago, and St. Louis Railroad operated out of a separate brick passenger depot on Third Street in Dayton in the late 1800s. Passenger use of this building ended with the opening of Union Station. To the left is another early design enclosed freight house. (Richard A. Lenehan collection.)

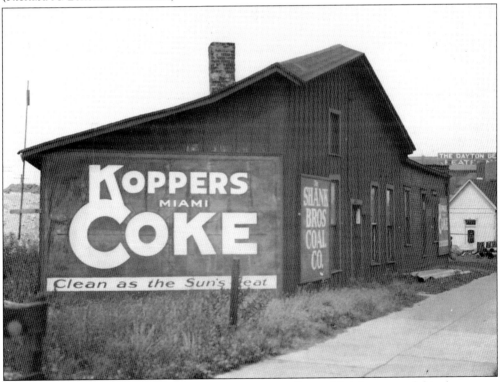

The Dayton and Southeastern, a former narrow-gauge line, sold tickets out of this depot near Third Street from 1877 until the early 1890s. The line was sometimes referred to as the "Black Diamond" line, since it stretched to the southeast Ohio coalfields. Other early Dayton depots stood at Webster and Third Streets and on West Third Street in Miami City. (Lutzenberger Photograph Collection, Dayton Metro Library.)

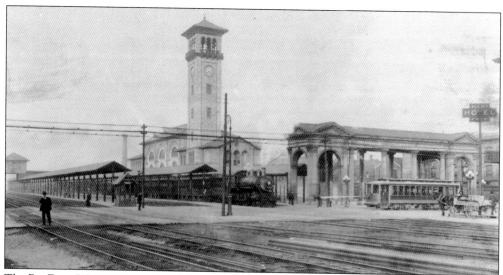

The Big Four, PCC&StL, and CH&D, under the guise of the Dayton Union Railway, dedicated a new Union Station just north of the old one July 27, 1901. The depot consisted of two buildings: one containing the waiting rooms, dining room, and lunchroom and the other housing baggage and express facilities. The second-floor areas contained railroad offices and a trainmen's waiting room. The prominent feature was a seven-story clock tower. Passengers were served on six through tracks. Note the terminal of the Dayton and Union Railroad just west of the station complex. (Above, Richard A. Lenehan collection; below, Lutzenberger Photograph Collection, Dayton Metro Library.)

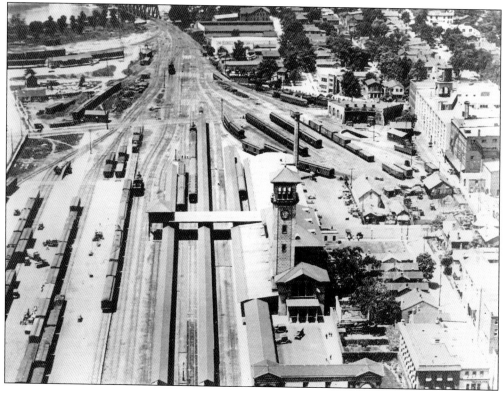

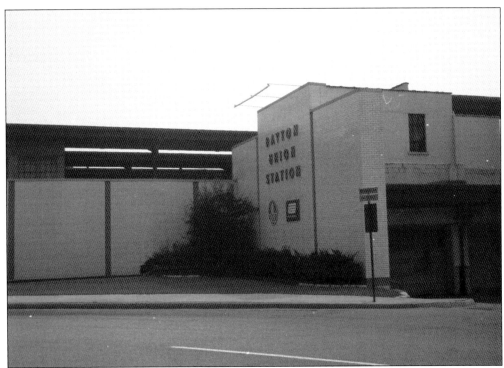

Tracks were elevated through the station complex between 1926 and 1931. In 1952, an annex was added to Union Station. Union Station was mostly demolished in spring-summer of 1964 when Sixth Street was to be extended. In September 1964, the new smaller depot shown here was dedicated. The last Amtrak passenger train, the National Limited, left the depot October 1, 1979. The remaining parts of Union Station were torn down in late 1988–early 1989. (Both, photographs by Charles Garvin.)

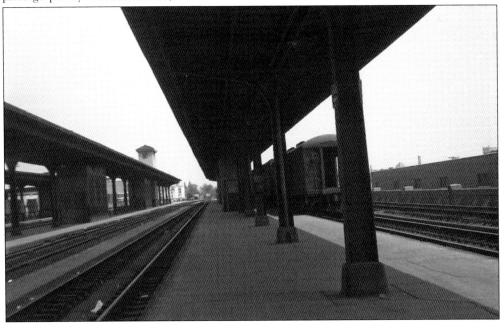

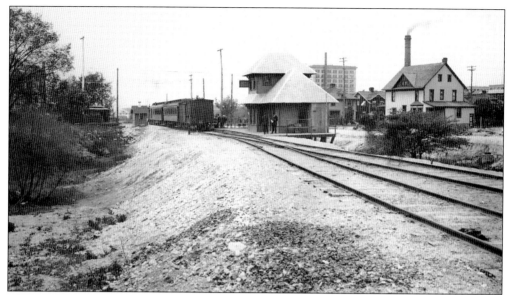

The Dayton, Lebanon, and Cincinnati Railroad and Terminal Company was organized in 1907 to extend the DL&C into downtown Dayton. In 1910, the Brown Street depot was opened. The above view shows a passenger train heading toward Dayton around 1910. Below, University of Dayton buildings form a backdrop for this c. 1913 view. The crossing watchman is for Brown Street. The DL&CR&T also built a passenger depot at Washington Street around 1912. (Both, Richard A. Lenehan collection.)

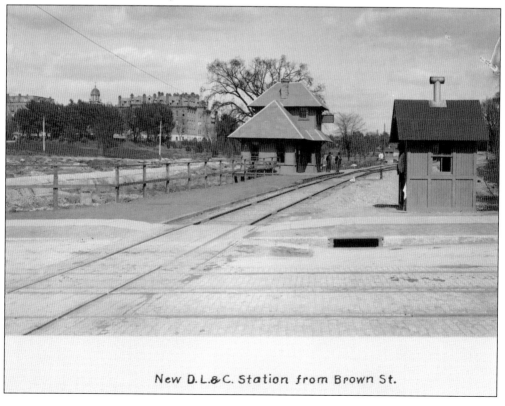

New D.L.&C. Station from Brown St.

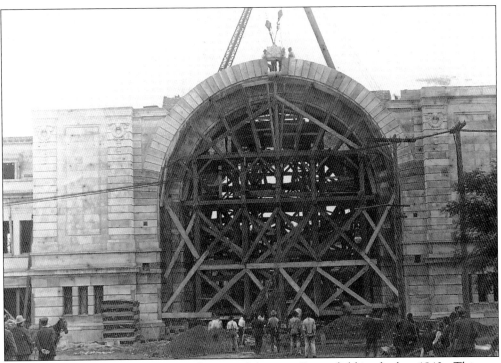

The Mad River and Lake Erie opened a second depot in Springfield in the late 1840s. This was replaced by a frame depot built between Limestone Street and Fountain Avenue. In 1910 (above), masons were completing the stonework arch of the Cleveland, Cincinnati, Chicago, and St. Louis Railway's new union station. The depot opened in 1911 east of the old depot. The old depot was demolished, and the site became known as Big Four Park. In just 15 years, the depot accommodated 26 daily passenger trains. In 1928, some 123,000 passengers used the depot. An open area below the second floor was enclosed to make more office space around 1940. The construction of the State Route 72 bypass led to the depot's demise in February 1969. Big Four Park is now a parking lot. (Both, author's collection.)

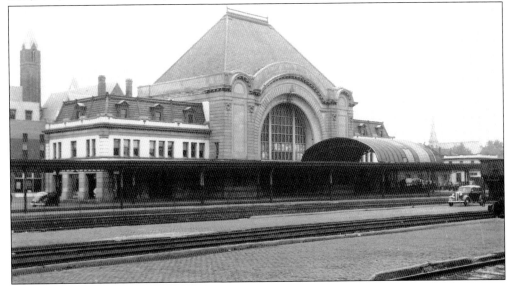

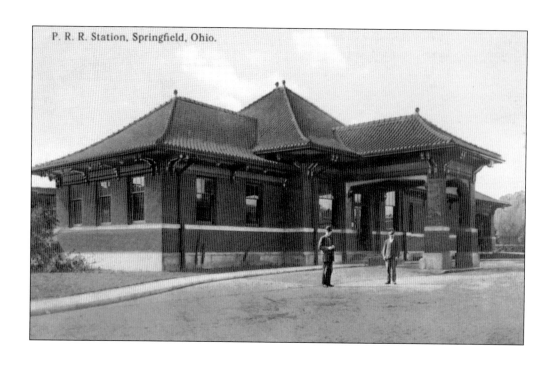

P. R. R. Station, Springfield, Ohio.

Adjoining the Big Four depot property were the brick depots of the PCC&StL Railroad. Predecessor Little Miami Railroad opened the first depot in Springfield arriving in 1846. The new PCC&StL depot was constructed to company plans around 1910 as part of the city's railroad improvements. Note that the passenger train up from Xenia will have to back out of the station grounds since the passenger track ends at the depot. (Above, author's collection; below, photograph by Richard A. Lenehan.)

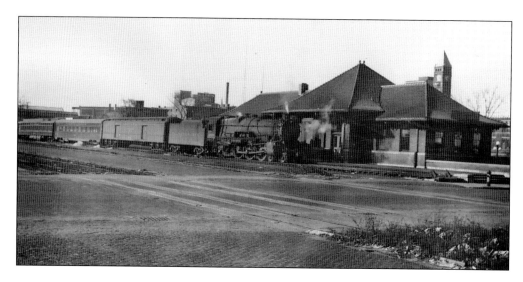

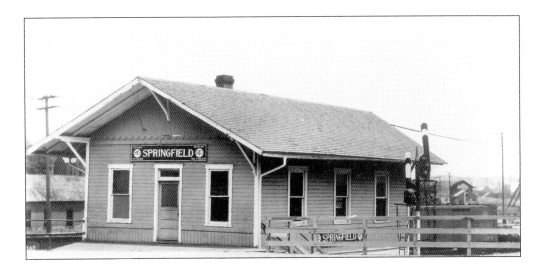

The Detroit, Toledo, and Ironton Railroad served the above two-story depot on North Limestone Street in Springfield near the PCC&StL and Big Four depots. Adjacent was a large brick freight house. Passenger service was discontinued at this depot in 1937 and shifted to the DT&I's large freight house on Burt Street. From 1931 to the end of all passenger service in 1954, mixed trains were run. The Erie Railroad depot below was erected in the late 1890s at the crossing of the DT&I on the northwest side of town. This diamond became known as Maitland in 1903. Directly across the tracks was a standard design Erie interlocking tower. (Above, Eldon Neff collection; below, Erie Railroad photograph, author's collection.)

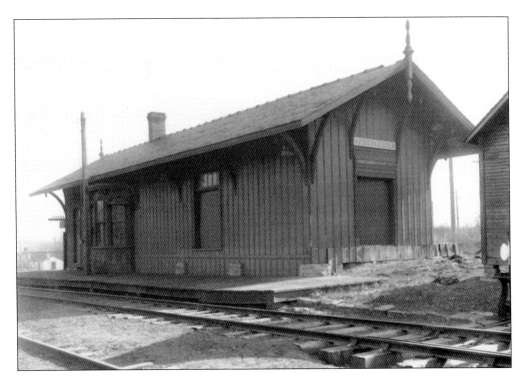

DISCOVER THOUSANDS OF LOCAL HISTORY BOOKS
FEATURING MILLIONS OF VINTAGE IMAGES

Arcadia Publishing, the leading local history publisher in the United States, is committed to making history accessible and meaningful through publishing books that celebrate and preserve the heritage of America's people and places.

Find more books like this at
www.arcadiapublishing.com

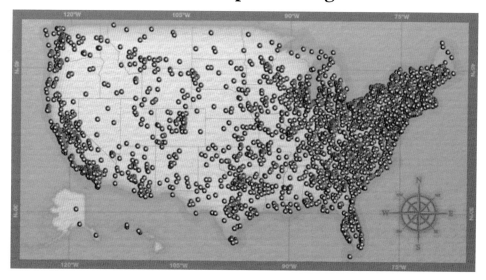

Search for your hometown history, your old stomping grounds, and even your favorite sports team.

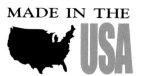